How
business
is

BAMBOOZLED

by the
Ad-Boys

How
business
is

BAMBOOZLED

by the
Ad-Boys

BY NICHOLAS SAMSTAG
INTRODUCTION BY ERIC HODGINS

JAMES H. HEINEMAN, INC., NEW YORK H

First Printing 1966

Library of Congress Catalogue Card Number: 65-26958.
© 1966 James H. Heineman, Inc., New York.
For information address: James H. Heineman, Inc., 60 East
42nd Street, New York, New York 10017

Printed and bound in the United States of America.

This book has been felicitously illustrated
by
Leo Glueckselig

FOREWORD

NOT LONG AGO my wife and I spent a month in Egypt. At Luxor, a couple of hundred miles up the Nile where there are several temples and the tombs of a lot of Pharaohs, we stopped at a huge hotel built by the British toward the beginning of the century. Thanks to Nasser, it is run by Egyptians now, and when we asked for our bill, something happened that provides a most appropriate springboard for this book.

There was a very large mistake on the bill—in *our,* not in the hotel's, favor. We were being vastly undercharged. I tried to explain it to the cashier who, until that moment, seemed to have spoken adequate English. But he kept shaking his head and finally called the manager, so I explained again. I couldn't get it: Why wouldn't these two see that they were gypping themselves of at least half their rightful due? Besides, I felt silly, as one always does when one is working too hard to give one's money away.

Finally, Mahmout, the *concierge,* came over and stood quietly listening for a moment. Then he tapped my shoulder and drew me aside.

"Pay, please?" he suggested with lifted eyebrows and his dazzling, white-toothed smile. "It will be easier. They do not wish to be wrong." And so there, on the site of ancient Thebes, we paid an establishment much less than it rightly deserved because it preferred to be underpaid rather than admit that its system was inefficient.

Face is not a thing peculiar to the East. Reading the pages that follow, the freshman in the business world (and there are many perennial freshmen there, some of them board chairmen) may well ask, "Why do advertisers tolerate such stupidity and skulduggery in both their agencies and their inside advertising departments?" The answer was propounded a few winters back by Mahmout at the Winter Palace Hotel: "It is easier. They do not wish to be wrong."

Too many businessmen who control the advertising of their companies have for too long been tolerating too many things. They have a deeply vested interest in not admitting that they have been wrong—they are more interested in *being* right about face than in doing one.

If you have a natural aptitude for some activity, you can accomplish a great deal by the exercise of it without working very hard. Work a little harder, of course, and you'll accomplish more. Work like mad at it and you may make history.

If, on the other hand, you aren't especially gifted at something, you can work at it like a monomaniac and you'll still produce only mediocrity. You'll end up all pooped out with nothing much to show for it.

Now, if you had to hire one of the following two candidates to work for you in advertising, which would you choose: a fellow with a gift for the trade but no great affection for hard work or a fellow with little aptitude for it who would knock himself out trying? If you'd choose the first candidate (as I would), you'll probably like this book. If you'd choose the second, you probably won't.

For, in preferring the man who will work harder whether or not he has any talent, you are showing that your attitude toward what you do (and probably toward all productive human activity) is fundamentally a religious one based on some form of Calvin's precept that there is an inherent worth in hard work. And, in that sense, this is an irreligious book about advertising, one that honors the cat more than the mule, results and grace rather than effort and sweat.

What has religion got to do with advertising? Plenty. Discuss this book's chapter on research with almost any marketing man you know and account for the bulging eyes, the throbbing temporal arteries, the intemperate language on any grounds other than that you have attacked his religion. Try the chapter on the ignorance of businessmen about advertising on some large advertiser who is not, himself, a professional ad man and note how the growing ruddiness of his complexion suggests that you are toying with his gods. Try the section that says most advertisements are written to be okayed (not to sell things) on almost any group of conservative men in business and hear the author get drummed out of the regiment as if he had been guilty of conduct unbefitting a gentleman.

It is not news that a great many Americans regard business as they should regard Christ or Jehovah, Mohammed or Buddha.

Their offices are where they worship, not their churches. And it isn't Money—it isn't Mammon who occupies the inner shrine; it's *Business*. It's the ritual of Titan and Status, of expense account and of who gets invited to the boss' house on weekends. Making money isn't the object of all this effort; it's only the *excuse* for it. For, if their major purpose was to make money, they wouldn't stand for all those sacred cows wasting their sustenance all over the place.

This transference is, in the author's opinion, a bad thing. And it is nowhere (except, possibly, in the automobile business in Detroit) as rife as in the advertising business. Let us render unto Caesar the things that are Caesar's and unto God the things that are God's. Advertising is of the market, not of the cathedral. It belongs not to God but to Caesar, and not just to Gaius Julius. Some of it, in fact, is clearly Caligula's. This book tries to make that clear.

So, dear reader, if anyone is going to be read out of the church, ask not for whom the bell tolls.

N.S.

Downhill-on-the-Ridge

ACKNOWLEDGMENTS

THE AUTHOR wishes to express his thanks to Williston C. Rich Jr., for his help in organizing this book and for his contributions to the chapter on the public relations of advertising; to Eric Hodgins for his Introduction and his enlightening (if sometimes barbed) suggestions on the text; to Leo Glueckselig for his zany and pertinent illustrations; to Edward L. Bernays for his sage suggestions on publicity relating the book to various "foci of beneficent infection"; to Carl Rogers, publisher of *Madison Avenue,* for permission to use portions of articles that first appeared in that magazine; to Suzanne Samstag, agency copywriter extraordinary, for doing the index and providing some excellent ideas that led to some really spectacular squabbles; to Mimi Rogers Weddell for her patient and accurate typing and retyping; and to Howard Gossage for his amiable, acidulous comments.

Finally, the author must record his indebtedness to advertising itself, which has fed and clothed him (albeit reluctantly) for lo, these many years. A treacherous and unstable provider, it has had to be tweaked, prodded and beaten continuously before yielding him an excellent livelihood, in return for which his outstanding emotion is not so much gratitude as triumph—and a *soupçon* of affection for the surly bitch.

N.S.

TABLE OF CONTENTS

DELUSION I

Nobody has ever successfully described Helen of Troy, nor would we be any nearer to an adequate description were it to be established beyond all reasonable doubt that her dimensions were 38-22-36.

DELUSION II

"Take a letter, Miss Preakness. To Fairfield Cheapside President, Cheapside, Fewlett, Inc. You know the address. Ready?

Dear Freddie: Joe Bilkim will be sixty years old on May fifteenth and I think it would be nice to show his photograph in all our advertising that month. The angle can be 'A Company Is Only As Good As the Man Who Heads It Up' and you can lay it on thick. After all—"

DELUSION III

The agency puts your money where it will do you the most good 43

"They send those engineers out from Toronto to ask me if I think the road ought to change over from steam to oil. Are they crazy? Here I've spent forty years learning how to run a steam-powered railroad and they ask me a question like that!"—Remark attributed to the western manager of the Union Pacific Railroad, circa 1935.

DELUSION IV

Too much attention is being paid to creativity and not enough to marketing 57

"Wait a minute!" said the Devil. "I've surveyed those other universes and only 11.9 per cent want a new solar system created. In fact 42.3 per cent said they would go somewhere else if you persist in this Garden of Eden stuff and—"

"Go away," said the Lord. "I'm busy."

DELUSION V

People buy for reasons of logic 69

"People will buy it for all sorts of reasons, many of which they won't understand themselves, but we'll have to give them socially acceptable motives that they can verbalize. When the wife or the boss or their son asks, 'Why did you buy that one?' our customers must have an answer. And so we've got

to get going on a *Here's Why You Bought It* folder
to enclose with every unit we sell."

ad man and only 4 per cent would like an ad man as a next-door neighbor. (7 per cent preferred "someone in retailing.")—Advertising Age, *May 5, 1961*

It is a corollary of the free market that no supplier can be blamed for meeting a demand. If, as in the sale of narcotics, so doing is against the public welfare, it is the government's duty to make the satisfaction of the demand illegal and to frustrate such satisfaction. But, until that time, the supplier is blameless.

INTRODUCTION

SINCE THIS IS A book of *caveats,* let me get mine in first thing: Watch Samstag.

I have been watching Samstag for a number of years. The results have been rich, in variety. I have been gratified, rewarded, victimized and appalled. I don't know how anyone could ask for more, or why he would want to.

Samstag is not "an advertising man." Instead he is his own man, and it must be this unusual quality which makes this book the first book on or about advertising I have ever been able to read without lower back pain, disillusionment and nausea. Being a member of the public, I have often been bamboozled by the authors of other books on advertising; often, in the sorrowing words of H. L. Mencken, been rolled, bounced and made a mock of. The implication has always been that some advertising mogul, the force of whose words has sold more imperial gallons of grain neutral spirits or moved more tons of cellucotton than ever since the Athens of Pericles, is now about to reveal his *mystique;* about to rend the last veil and show everyone how things are done. Well, second only to pornography, from which these revelations must be delicately distinguished, the confessions of advertising men make the dullest reading within the grasp of movable types. The advertising man, writing his own book instead of sticking to his own last, which is very different, cannot sustain for two chapters the illusion that he is going to give away useful trade secrets. Instead, after the opening chapters, the confessioning ad man tries to fob off on you his life's philosophy. It turns out he can't deliver on this, either: Dr. Norman Vincent Peale has already uttered all his deeper thoughts, sometimes anticipating him by a remarkable span of years.

This is not that kind of book at all. The reader may not like everything in it; I don't myself, but I consider it well worth the money. It does not describe advertising, it does not explain advertising, it does not beatify advertising, it does not exemplify advertising. It *challenges* advertising, and most particularly the advertising man and his advertising credos. It walks right up to the Archbishops of Madison Avenue and says Boo to them in their chancels, whereupon all their clothes fall off. Unlike other writers, Samstag did not promise a peep show. He gives you, instead, an eyeful. It is, as Scotland Yard must have said of Jack the Ripper, a bit unsettling.

Nevertheless, it must be read. The uneasy priests of advertising work very hard at their mythology, but they know something

about it they wish they didn't: They know they invented it. They have been smarter than their clients, until now; therefore they are acutely conscious that they *could* be found out. It is not that they have said Yes when the true answer was No. It is that they have widely pretended and actively fostered the pretense that they were in possession of some unalterable first principles so sacred that they must not be questioned, or even openly discussed; since this was not in fact so, they found themselves under the necessity of creating diversion after diversion. Samstag's book is going to end most of this, I think, and make it evident to many businessmen who should have known it before, that advertising men are no more in exclusive and total possession of Truth than Baptists or psychoanalysts. As with these two other categories, they've got hold of something, all right, but they don't know what it is, and they are terribly afraid that efforts to find out might kill the goose that has been laid with golden eggs.

In addition to urging readers to read this book, I urge them also to read its successor which, so far as my knowledge goes, Samstag has not yet planned to write. Advertising forces much thought upon us; thus, today, I find myself thinking, alternately, about shaving preparations and whisky. I am told, for example, that Rapid Shave, a splendid product, doubtless, has seventeen different beard-softening ingredients. This is frightening, and has driven me to an electric shaver, which requires 110 volts, but not 110 *different* volts. If there are seventeen different beard-softeners in the solar system, I do not want the responsibility of pressing the valve to release them; tactical atomic weapons are as far as I go.

On the other hand, there are certain pot-still whiskies which, if uncontaminated by the addition of 65 per cent grain neutral spirits, contain at least seventeen different drunk-making ingredients. And I think it very odd that no distiller ever bases an advertising claim on the absolute reliability of his product in doing what he knows it will do. His is one of the few advertising classifications whose products never fail. But instead of taking advantage of this, he goes mooning around about flavor, aroma and body, plus veiled insinuations about his product and Sex—which could get him into *real* trouble if a stalwart plaintiff were ever to come forward and tell the unvarnished truth.

Oscillating between Rapid Shave, which doesn't shave at all but merely prepares, and soft hard liquor, a concept which confuses without intoxicating, I have been trying, like Euclid, to develop some Propositions; unlike Euclid, I am aware of their extreme frailty and that some exception can be found or taken to every one. But they do represent a beginning; Samstag is the man to carry on from here, someday, if he will:

PROPOSITION I: The advertising of Liquids provides a 90 per cent wider scope for mendacity than the advertising of Solids.

PROPOSITION II: If a Liquid, whether as solution, emulsion, colloid (sol or gel), is for use in any conjunction with human hair, any Claim is interchangeable with any other Claim.

PROPOSITION III: In proportion as a Solid becomes more and more insoluble in water or in stomach acids, or in resistance to combustion, the possibility of making a mendacious Claim for it decreases.

PROPOSITION IV: If the loci of a Product's use are the bathroom, the stomach, the kitchen, the face, the laundry, or the axilla, anything whatever may be said about it.

PROPOSITION V: The Claims made for a Product are inversely proportional to the cube of that Product's inability to fulfill them.

I hope younger and stronger hands may someday advance and refine what is here set forth. Indeed, Samstag seems often right on the verge of getting these things into proper form. Please read *this* book first, however: a boxed two-volume set is barely in the discussion phase.

I began this foreword with the injunction to watch Samstag. It is not unlike bird watching, except that you seldom need binoculars. Samstag the man is gentle, and says terrible things in a soft, well-modulated, conversational voice. He said something incredibly terrible to me several months ago, and I challenged him to look me straight in the eye and repeat it. He did. Then, because there is honesty in the man, he added, "But for your sake let me warn you not to confuse sincerity with self-control." Samstag doesn't, and I am trying not to.

ERIC HODGINS

NEW YORK, N. Y.
June 1965

4

THE ARGUMENT

An abyss of misunderstanding separates those who prepare advertising from the most powerful executive in the picture, the management man who pays for it. To appreciate the width of this abyss, listen to a monologue by the head of a business who has been working all day with his agency group and has been yessed from the morning coffee klatch through the late afternoon break for martinis. He feels trapped—by his own people as well as the agency. What's going on? What do they really think? "Why don't you ever tell me I'm wrong?" he inquires of no one in particular, and his monologue (it has echoed in thousands of lonely executive suites) goes something like this:

"You know I want to be told what you think about things. Why don't more of you speak up when you disagree with me? Sometimes I feel as if I'm running our advertising show in a vacuum. I can't know everything about advertising, can I? That's *your* specialty.

"Of course, when you think I'm wrong, give it to me easy. Once is enough; you don't have to say it over and over again. Furthermore, if you think I'm wrong two or three times a week, perhaps you ought to tell me about only one of those times.

"Another thing: There are acceptable ways of telling a client

when he's wrong and there are unacceptable ways. Take it easy.

"For example, a pretty good opening gambit is: 'I bet you'll see bugs in this one that I can't see.' Well, that's maybe a bit greasy, but you get the idea. It's certainly better than: 'That's a lousy idea!'

"How should I tell *you* when I think you're wrong? Well, send me a memo about that. But remember: It's your job to get along with me, not mine to get along with you.

"Or am I wrong?"

The answer to the client's final query is: "Not necessarily, but very likely." The man is simply the victim of a nervous breakdown in communication. His defensiveness shows like the slip of a slattern: He wants the truth and he doesn't; he is prepared to take it on the chin, but be careful: He has a glass jaw. And he isn't sure that he is handling his agency as it ought to be handled, with the right blend of toughness and consideration for creative sensibilities, the right combination of authority and receptiveness.

Obviously, the agency is too often afraid to say what it thinks for fear that it will lose the business. But behind this fear (which is present in the dealings of any supplier with any customer in any industry) is a more serious problem. For the businessman is separated from the advertising man by a great void of semantics. The two keep talking the same subject (advertising), but they do it in different languages. If some of the issues could be isolated and discussed in a common language, the first filaments of understanding might be flung across the gulf.

TWO IMPORTANT NOTES

1. On the language used in this book

While the issues separating the businessman and the advertising man should be discussed in a common language, this is not at all the same thing as a single idiom. The idioms of communication are many and, habitually, too few are used in any single work. For some people and some situations the idiom of the objective report is most effective. The more matter of fact and unadorned the idiom is, the better. But other problems and persons respond more sensitively to the idioms of literature: dramatization, narration, personal opinion, humor, even fantasy.

All idioms are used in this book. For when we must discuss subjects as touchy as whether a profession can have integrity, how a man feeds his vanity while calling his greediness something else, what does or does not constitute personal honesty, disillusionment, despair, we need all the tools we can get. The material we must deal with is like vegetation in a tropical rain forest: It slips from our grasp; it rests under our weight or it springs back and slaps us in the face with its thorny exceptions and contradictions.

And so a certain agility is required of the reader as he moves on through these pages. Let us, therefore, be patient with one another and hold each other's hands as we proceed.

2. On the section headings of the book

The sections into which this book is divided are headed, "Delusion I," "Delusion II," "Delusion III," etc. The words that follow—i.e. "The First Purpose of an Advertisement is to Sell Something"—are therefore, in the author's opinion, *untruths,* too often presented as truths by the ad man for reasons that will, he hopes, become clear.

A great deal of unnecessary confusion can be compounded in the reader's mind by his overlooking this essential fact, or by his forgetting it. To paraphrase Gertrude Stein, "A delusion is a delusion is a delusion"—so let's get it and keep it straight.

The section heads are *delusions.* All together now: *"Delusions = Not True!"*

Nobody has ever successfully described Helen of Troy, nor would we be any nearer to an adequate description were it to be established beyond all reasonable doubt that her dimensions were 38-22-36.

DELUSION I

"You can make good advertisements out of statistics"

O NCE UPON A TIME a Chicagoan named L. B. cornered the onion market. As a result, his firm made scallions of money and he became president.

For years afterwards, all his second-line executives tried to figure out how he had done it.

"He plotted the seasonal increase in mouthwash sales for the past ten years," said one, "and projected from there."

"It was those new private weather forecasters," insisted another. "He used to get daily reports from six of them on the growing weather all over the country and he extrapolated the figures from—"

"Nope," said a third. "It was the man's personal charm. Only ten growers are responsible for 78.4 per cent of all onion production. He got to know every one of them personally. He bought their kids birthday presents. Their wives were—"

But every time they asked L. B., "Is *this* the way you did it?" he shook his head. For, truth to tell, he didn't know *how* he'd done it; he was an intuitive type. And pretty soon they all began to say, "Aw, the hell with it. L. B. was just lucky."

That got him sore. He wanted people to think he was smart, not just sensitive. So he worked out a combination of all the systems that had been suggested to him, called a meeting of the Steering Committee at The Wagon Wheel in Rockton and announced, "Here is how I cornered the onion market. For the good of the firm, I want you all to know the secret, for I am getting old." Then he retired. And six months later he died—of a surfeit of chives, they said.

Time marched on. Two years later the firm's comptroller called another meeting, this time at the Drake Oakbrook.

"Look, everybody," he said that first night when the brandy was served after dinner. "All the factors that L. B. plotted in 1958 when he cornered the onion market are shaping up this year about the way they did then. We must go all out on onions. We should buy onions with *every cent we can get!*"

The Management Committee crowded around to look at his graphs and figures. He was right. They paralleled 1958 almost to the last bushel. So the boobies sold their bonds and their wives' jewelry and took a big loan at the bank—and they bought up all the onions they could get.

But something was wrong. There were new rapscallions in the market. Or there was a leek somewhere. The price of onions went down and down—and they all went broke.

For L. B. had been an artist, not a scientist. *But his colleagues just couldn't stand living with a truth like that.*

Advertising is also more an art than a science. But the men who pay for advertising are ill at ease in the presence of artists. They want "the facts, ma'am, just the facts." And to get the support of these men, most advertising agencies make believe that they build ads the way bridges are built, with logarithm tables—whereas they actually do their jobs with ouija boards.

This deception is practiced wherever business tries to treat human beings as if they were predictable robots. You can see management hiding behind phony statistics in much of its hiring and firing, in the company's relations with its community, in much of its internal communications. It is not only in advertising that we find an excessive, compulsive (and irrelevant) dependence on figures.

Those figures are management's out. In assembling them, the professional manager gathers alibis while he may—in advance. He knows that if everything goes to pot, he can show the directors and shareholders how conscientiously he marshaled his facts before he made his wrong decisions. He is like the lawyer who takes hours to explain your case to you (at a base rate of $50 an hour) and then asks you to choose between several possible courses—adroitly ducking the responsibility you hired him to assume.

Few decisions involving the way in which human beings will act can be made from statistics—and the experienced manager knows this. Intuition almost always plays the major role, and it is for the top manager's intuition, as much as anything else, that the shareholders pay him. Why then, does he not make his decisions intuitively? The answer is that the best managers do, but they present their decisions to their employers the way the ad agencies do to their clients: as if they had been made with slide rules.

Seductio ad absurdum

Don't let the pie charts and research mumbo-jumbo fool you. An *advertisement is a seduction*. It can be successful or unsuccessful, in good or bad taste. But it cannot be created with any technique based chiefly on mathematics. There are no objective standards against which the efficacy of a seduction can be measured in advance. If it is a successful seduction, it wins everybody's approval; the girl isn't merely seduced; she's fulfilled. If it is unsuccessful, the seducer will be punished by the loss of customers previously obtained by effective seductions and repelled by his awkward or tasteless advertising blunders.

Often, it is more the tone of voice that counts—the style, the way in which the presentation is made than any other factor. It is a matter of manner more than matter—and this is so at any age.

Berelson and Steiner in *Human Behavior* (Harcourt, Brace & World) observe that: "By and large, the pervasive emotional tone used by parents in raising their children affects subsequent development more than the techniques of child-rearing (e.g. permissiveness, restrictiveness, punishment, reward or the cohesiveness of the family unit)."

And, close to the opposite extreme, we all know what a magically compassionate way some executives have of telling older men in the firm that they should soon begin to think of retirement. The results obtained by these gentle men compare tragically with those of their less sensitive (or less gifted) colleagues who so often turn the firm's proud old pros into humiliated geriatric wrecks. Using almost precisely the same words, the younger superior will in one case have the tone of a senator talking to an elder statesman, in the other that of a brash young cop shooing a dirty old man off the street.

Seduction is part of our way of life in America. It goes by many names: "charm," "personality," "appeal," "glamour," "charisma." We are seduced into taking jobs, joining religious sects, working for political candidates. We seduce others—lots of others if we're effective, few if we're not. The mind can be seduced as well as the heart. So can the intestines, for that matter.

Artists, not technicians, are the best seducers. They deal in effects that may or may not be truths. Artists, in or out of truth, specialize in color, form, tone, line, emphasis, timing—not in facts, surveys, budgets, data.

Somewhere in their neighborhood (a little to the right and a few steps to the rear) is the place of the technicians in advertising. They have their function, but it is not the creation of advertisements. And a most important aspect of that function is to keep out of the hair of the creative man while he is producing advertisements.

A Better Class of Squirrels

The author wasn't sure of the statements that follow while he was an organization man. Or, if he was, he lacked the courage to make them, for they undermine the foundations of a theory of advertising created by the top operating executives of large companies to bolster their own decisions—and it is a dangerous thing to deprive one's superiors of their alibis. But since he has hung out his own shingle, he has found such agreement with these statements in high places that there is no longer any doubt in his mind that they are true. One of the many advantages in moving from an executive suite to a park bench is that you can talk with a better class of squirrels there. What follows is the distillation of a succession of ruminative conversations with some superior organization squirrels who talked to me frankly for the first time only after I had ceased to be one of them.

They feel, as do I, that business must find a new way of thinking about and understanding people. If we ever do find this ultimate way, it may turn out to be not technological at all, but rather an art or a combination of technology and art. For the great and growing area of advertising called marketing seems, like sociology, always to be squinting—trying to shut out the dazzle of all the many things people are in order to measure just one kind of thing that a certain group of them might be at a certain moment.

What Do They Really Want?

For example, there are three people who appear in any marketing situation: the *Instigator,* for whom the marketing project is being conducted (usually the Advertiser); the *Technician,* or market researcher, who directs the project (usually employed by the Agency), and the *Target,* who is the buyer, user or prospect— sometimes a member of the public, sometimes a businessman or a member of a profession. A host of marketing problems arises from the tendency to view these three as if they were machines, each with a single mechanical purpose—like a potato peeler, a pipe reamer, or a bottle capper.

We think of the Instigator, for instance, as if his chief purpose were to sell more of his product. That is almost assuredly a faulty view of most Instigators. One of their purposes, no doubt, *is* to sell more of their products, but here are five things in which any instigator may be more interested than the one we wrongly assume to be at the top of his priority list. All of these motives, of course, are motivations of personal gain, for there are no others. We strive sometimes for psychological, sometimes for material rewards, but always for personal gain.

Our Instigator, for example, if he is vice president in charge of marketing, may want to prove that a competing vice president is wrong more than he may want to increase the sale of his product. Or he may want to show that a service or material supplied by a friend is badly needed in the manufacture or sale of his product, so that he can throw a contract to that friend. (Remember all those executives in the electrical machinery field who were jailed a few years ago?) He may be more interested in wanting to make a reputation for himself as a daring operator than in making a profit for his company or in trying to sell his product to more people under better conditions. He may want, prayerfully and desperately, to prove that his boss, the president or the chairman of the board, is right in order to butter his bread thicker. Or he may simply want to show that an opinion he has expressed for many years within his company remains sound, and that he is *not* an old, out-of-date fuddy-duddy.

He may want to achieve any or all of these things and an infinitude of others more than he wants the only goal you attribute to him, to sell more of his product. The Instigator, in short, is not a machine for finding more profitable ways of selling his product. He is a whole man—with a most unpredictable priority list of motivations.

Motives Are Seldom Visible

Now, take our second character, the Technician or Market Researcher working for the advertising agency. If asked for a generalized description of his purpose, one might say: "He is a man dedicated to searching out every way of finding the best possible market for his product or service." On the other hand he may be mainly concerned with making a big marketing reputation for himself. Or he may want to please the Instigator of the survey or some officer of the agency at any cost, or get himself a trip to Europe, or make a lot of money. And he may want any of these things far more than he wants to find the best possible market for his product or service.

And, of course, the third member of our trinity, the Buyer, Prospect or User, has an awful lot of things on his mind other than the one objective most of us tag him with. He does not necessarily want the most for his money. He may want a Pontiac, regardless, because someone he once admired when he was younger drove one. Rather than the safest airplane he can take, he may, because of a subconscious death wish, be attracted to the ones that have been cracking up lately. (Erich Fromm, in *Escape From Freedom*, claimed that the entire German nation suffered from an urge to self-destruction.) And, instead of the best television set for the money, it may be that he doesn't want a TV set at all; he is more interested in seeming to be a highbrow.

The Culture Bluffers

While we're on TV, I guess it is no secret now that there are people who do not tune in the kind of programs they are constantly demanding. They ask for culture and watch *Bonanza*. Aw-

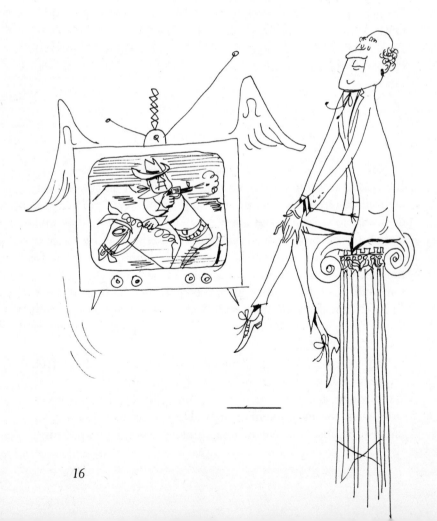

fully human of them, isn't it? But it speaks eloquently of the failure of a certain kind of superficial research.

There are thousands of hypotheses that can be tested in any survey, and years can be spent in running through them methodically. Or you can focus on one or a few in order to do a survey quickly.

And that is where research in advertising becomes authoritarian. It chooses a few motives and assumes that these are the major ones to measure against one another.

I remember that in the early days of electric shavers I suspected a profound truth which none of the research seemed to disclose. It was that once you get a man to buy an electric shaver he is almost immediately a terrific prospect for another electric shaver. That may sound silly, but hold still a moment: (1) The customer bought one of these early electric shavers and couldn't get a good shave with it (2) He felt like a dope for having spent $15 on one (3) His wife noticed the absence of the electric hum after the first week and began to needle him for having wasted his money (4) He immediately became a prospect for a later, "improved" electric shaver (namely, the newest model advertised) so that he could "save face" with the little woman.

In those days there were scores of men with four and five electric shavers cached in their top bureau drawers. They had bought one after the other in hope of getting a decent shave without backtracking to the old safety razor method. Because they would not admit that they were wrong to buy an electric shaver in the first place, they were the industry's best prospects. But you would never have known this from the research. We found it out by running an ad (with coupon) headlined, DON'T LET HER BEARD YOU IN YOUR DEN! Because it *pressed the nerve that hurt*, the real reason why shaver owners were the best prospects for new models, it outpulled every other coupon ad we ever ran—four to one.

How Do You Measure Bounce?

There are many things in life that cannot be proved, and it is best to admit it. Let's call those that can be weighed, measured and proved "things of substance," in contrast with "things of the spirit," which are abstract, imponderable, unprovable. Here, for example, are some paired statements. The first part of each has to do with substance; the second part with spirit:

Contrast "He bought her a diamond ring"—with "He loves her dearly." . . . Contrast "He never misses a Sunday at church" —with "He's a truly religious person." . . . Contrast "He's worked overtime every night this week"—with "He always has the good of the company at heart."

In each of these contrasts, the first statement can be proved, the second cannot. You see the diamond ring; you can *find* him at church on Sundays; you can *check* our hero's overtime. But how are you going to look into his heart to find if "he loves her dearly," or measure his true spirituality or his true loyalty to his company? And yet, on the answers to these unprovable questions depend the most important relationships in a man's life: his relationship with his family, his soul and his work.

Would anyone deny that the things of spirit in these questions are every bit as important as the things of substance? I think that most Americans would agree that a man's love for his wife is more important than the objects he buys for her, that his attitude toward his immortal soul is more significant than the time he spends in church, and that the depth of his sincerity in behalf of his company is more meaningful than the hours he spends at his desk.

Let's narrow the focus and apply these concepts to the theory and practice of advertising. When one thinks of the great advertising appeals of our day, how about this matter of substance versus spirit? Is the emphasis on the one or the other—on the provable or the unprovable?

How about "They Satisfy"? Chesterfield could have based its famous theme on measurable, ponderable, comparable things. It could have focused on the amount of Latakia in the tobacco, emphasized the length of time it takes to smoke a Chesterfield (a "Longer Smoke-Pleasure"), stressed the relative rigidity of the Chesterfield package compared to the collapsibility of competing packages. But Chesterfield says simply: "They Satisfy"—and millions have agreed that they do, accepting the fact, although "Satisfaction" is, of course, *scientifically unprovable*.

How about "The Beer that Made Milwaukee Famous"? Should beer get the credit at all? I am told that beer accounts for only 5 per cent of Milwaukee's labor force. And Schlitz is only one of three Milwaukee beers with national distribution! The statement is unproved.

And so is Pepsi-Cola's "More Bounce to the Ounce." What in the devil is "bounce"? How do you measure it? There's Barnum and Bailey's "The Greatest Show on Earth." Who says so? And "Salem's Softness Freshens the Taste" may be, even without the music, the Mt. Everest of mellifluous, seductive vacuity.

You can name dozens of such appeals: renowned advertising slogans, lines, copy themes, which have demonstrated their effectiveness over the years—appeals which refer to abstractions, or appeals that are statements about things as unprovable as love, loyalty or any other human quality.

"Unprovable" Is Not "Untrue"

In fact, after many years spent in measuring only physical, countable, provable things like people's incomes and possessions, research itself has finally turned toward honoring spirit as well as substance. It has moved into the field of *motivational inquiry* where its findings are truly unprovable.

Notice, please, that I said "unprovable," not "untrue." Motivational research has become advertising's arsenal of "the truths that can't be proved." Every day its practitioners come up with unarguable truths. They are truths about people: why people do or do not do things, and why people feel as they do.

It may be true that a woman takes a cake out of her oven and looks at it in the same spirit of tremulous pride and questioning with which she first examines a newborn child that she has produced. It may be that when a man buys his first convertible he feels as if he is taking a mistress. And it may also be that some very effective advertisements can be written around these discoveries. But their truth just cannot be proved.

The immortal jurist, Oliver Wendell Holmes, once said, with the simplicity that was his mark, "If a law makes you want to puke, then due process has been denied." Conversely, when a fact of substance seems right and sound, when it makes you feel its integrity, you can almost always be sure it is right because it supports a higher truth, a truth of the spirit.

In fact, the successful motivational researcher builds his whole reputation on his feeling for the intuitive truth. To succeed, such a man must possess superior sensitivity, education, wisdom and experience. He cannot be a dolt about statistics. He must also be a man of expediency who sells his personal opinions to his clients under the guise of research *services,* the mechanics of measuring. He must practice this largely harmless deceit rather than waste his sustenance in a ceaseless fight against the bullheaded stupidity of the management man who hires him.

When such an executive has a pain in his gut, he trots to his internist, who often sends him to some diagnostician who charges a justifiably high fee. In their first interview, the specialist probably tells him in all honesty that he must undergo certain tests involving his blood, liver, uric acid or cholesterol and that these tests will cost him so much money. Then, says the specialist, he will give "an opinion." And that is just what the man does. There is no pretense that his fee is a bill for tests. It's a bill for an opinion —an educated guess, based on the doctor's sensitivity, education, wisdom, talent and experience. A charge for the tests is also made, but that is a minor sum.

When the same process takes place, however, with a market or a product substituting for the tycoon's gut, hardly a researcher now alive dares to render his bill as, "One thousand interviews at $2.00—$2,000.00. Diagnosis—$8,000.00. Total—$10,000.00." Oh no. The bill reads: "One thousand interviews made by specially trained, psychologically oriented interviewers on a sample of the universe based on the McGarry-Shiefflin formula of extrapolated averages at $10.00 each—$10,000.00."

And that is OK with the president. He, who is himself supposedly paid by the stockholders to use his judgment, often refuses to pay a market researcher for using his, thus forcing the man to bury his fee in the price of a lot of fancy-sounding measurements.

No Reason Why for Caesar

Now let us return to the authoritarian role of technological research in advertising, especially as it applies to marketing. It should be obvious that the specific hypothesis is to research in the field of science what the specific written advertisement is to research in the field of advertising. It is fruitless for a scientist embarking on a research project to set out without some assumption, some proposition whose truth or falsity he will attempt to discover. Merely to venture forth to see what he will find is a feckless endeavor, for the possibilities are too numerous to handle. He must set out to prove or disprove *something* or there will be no direction and no end to his investigations. So it is in advertising research. Some specific advertisement must first be created. Only then is there something to test or measure in the marketplace.

Why is this so? Why cannot researchers seek out the susceptibilities of the market, the reasons why people need and buy a product—and having found them, why can they not *then* build their advertisements around the most promising of the susceptibilities? Well, one reason is that there exists an infinite number of market susceptibilities for almost any product, as well as an infinity of possible advertisements that can be written around each one of them. So infinity is piled upon infinity until reels the mind.

But another and more important reason is that it may not be possible to get a good advertisement written around the susceptibilities that win a researcher's sweepstakes. The fact is that it is much, much harder to write a good advertisement than to locate a promising susceptibility. So everybody keeps trying for the good advertisement, and it is only when one finally appears that the researchers can go to work.

Does anyone think seriously that the "I'm a Homely Little Lamp" Tensor ad was written as a result of market research? Did his director of research summon Commander Whitehead full-bearded from the brow of David Ogilvy? Did the sober-sided slide-rulers have anything much to do with "While You're Up, Get Me a Grant's"? I doubt it.

What actually happened in these cases was that some creative character with perhaps very little knowledge of the product or the market, but with a sure instinct of what will interest and persuade people, wove an unexpected, unlikely and unforgettable spell. And *then* the researchers proved that it would catch the eye and charm the mind—and sell lamps, beards, Schweppervescence or Grant's whisky to Americans in highly satisfactory quantity.

They might have proved that it wouldn't. All that glitters is not gold, and many a deliciously composed and expertly tied trout fly draws no strikes because it is cast in the wrong stream, in the wrong way, or at the wrong time of year. When this occurs, there follows in the studies of the researchers an ominous

pause—while everybody waits for another promising advertisement to be created. The technicians take the day (or the month) off.

It is obvious that Cleopatra would have gotten nowhere using a statistical reason-why approach on Antony. Or on Caesar. And so it is also with the advertiser. Let us, therefore, render unto Cleo the things that are hers, and to Caesar the things that are hisn.

The Frogginess of Frogs

C. P. Snow has observed that our world has split into two cultures, and that these cultures have been growing further and further apart since the scientific revolution. He says that a great gulf exists today between the men of science and the rest of us, especially those who are called literary or intellectual. Too many scientists, says Snow, speak their own language, have their own disciplines, know nothing and care less about the rest of the world where formulas, scientific procedures and mathematical equations do not rule—and where novels are read, music is listened to, and instinct and emotion are pre-eminent.

I doubt that he has ever read the *Advertising Research Journal*, but it would certainly snow C. P. Snow. Tons and tons of jargon tumble forth, and not an ounce of insight. The approach of the operations researchers is a menace to the entire business of marketing. Susceptible souls in and around marketing are being packed into the mathematical approach as if it were the Black Hole of Calcutta—and they will smother to death there.

After you dissect the frog, after you memorize the Latin names of all its organs, muscles, nerves, and how they relate to one another, you still know nothing about the "frogginess of frogs." To become a frog expert you must spend sunny days and rainy nights, summer evenings and winter dawns observing him in his own world, with his friends and enemies, diseases and amusements, his children, and his long moments of motionless reverie. And then, after you know him whole almost as well as you know yourself, you still can't describe him scientifically—you must do it, if at all, in a poem or a story or a picture.

And that is what good research should be—a way of helping the intuitive man, the whole man, to understand his market *in the round;* a way of helping him live with the frogs so that he can, by seeing them whole, be more intuitive, more creative about them; so that his imagination can be freed.

Too often, marketing in its misguided role as policeman and nothing else, says: "You *can't* do this; you *can't* do that. Your prospect is merely *this;* your customer is precisely *that.*"

Marketing should be an emancipator. It should unlock locks and cut bonds by suggesting and implying, by hinting and beckoning, not by defining. It should be the agent that frees, not the agent that imprisons. "Why not try this? Why not do that? Have you thought that they may be buying for these reasons? Don't forget your market is also this, also that."

In brief, we need more and more affirmative, plastic, humanistic, refreshing research, less and less scientistic authoritarianism. And there are signs that advertising is going to get it.

Forward, researchers! *You have nothing to lose but your dogma.*

*"Take a letter, Miss Preakness. To Fairfield
Cheapside, President, Cheapside, Fewlett, Inc.
You know the address. Ready?
Dear Freddie: Joe Bilkim will be sixty years old on
May fifteenth and I think it would be nice to show
his photograph in all our advertising that month.*
The angle can be 'A Company Is Only As Good
As the Man Who Heads It Up' *and you can lay it
on thick. After all—"*

DELUSION II

"The first purpose of an advertisement is to sell something"

FEWER AND FEWER PEOPLE work just for money any more. Fewer and fewer people eat just for nourishment, go abroad just to broaden their minds, buy cars just for transportation, make love just to have babies. And more and more people admit it.

And fewer and fewer advertisements are published just to sell merchandise.

These observations were triggered by an article I read recently about the difference between the Chicago school of advertising and the New York school of advertising. *What a lot of balderdash!* After pointing out that there wasn't any difference and thus protecting himself, the author quoted a gaggle of top Chicago and New York ad men who, for the most part, claimed that there *are* differences. The Chicago school (surprise!) is supposed to be blunter and harder sell. The New York school (astonishment!) is supposed to be subtler, wittier, more interested in trying to get an advertisement admired than a product sold. But the article's author seemed to feel that the only question was how to get the product sold; you were either faithful or unfaithful to this creed. Bah!

Advertising's basic law of thermodynamics is that *the first purpose of an advertisement is to get itself read. The second purpose is a secret.*

How do you know *why* an advertisement is published? Once upon a time, when the author worked for a large weekly newsmagazine, the president of a Midwestern soup company came to town (something he seldom did) and was invited to lunch in the publication's executive dining rooms by the magazine's advertising director. After a repast more Lucullan than usual, Harry got up and made a short, graceful speech, thanking Mr. Slurp for the twelve-month schedule of spreads he'd been running in full color with various menu suggestions.

"We know that our publication is read by more than a million women with higher than usual standards and incomes," said Harry, "and it's nice to have an advertiser like you in the book, talking to our women as housewives and mothers."

After Harry was finished, Mr. Slurp arose. "I hate to think that I've had all those martinis and eaten all that good food under false pretenses," he said, "but we've been advertising with you because we're going to float a new stock issue soon and we wanted to keep our name in front of the investors in your readership. We couldn't figure any better way to do it than to act as if we were trying to sell soup."

All Hail Mr. Slurp!

Although Mr. Slurp's disclosure somewhat discomfited his host, it perfectly exemplifies a simple fact. An advertisement may not always be trying to sell what it *seems* to be trying to sell, but it must always satisfy *somebody* before it appears, and I don't mean the consumer. I mean the man who must approve the ad; in this case, probably Mr. Slurp. The best way to satisfy this somebody is often the best way to sell something. But that is not always true; it may not even be *mostly* true.

An anecdote which illustrates clearly what I mean concerns a well-known advertising man who was at the time chief executive officer of a formidable advertising agency. He had been trying for three years to land a big, profitable account, and things looked very promising when, one morning, the prospect phoned and asked him to drop over.

That afternoon, in the prospect's office, the fruit of three years' courtship dangled in the balance. The talk went on. "What happens," the prospect asked, "if we don't like Barton, Rubicam & Belding's idea for some major campaign of ours?"

"We will submit our *second* best idea," said the ad man.

"And if we don't like *that* one?"

"We will then," said our hero suavely, "show you our *third* best idea."

But the prospect wasn't letting him off that easy. "What," he inquired, giving him the hard eye, "if we don't like *any* of your damned ideas, but like our own better?"

"In that case," replied the imperturbable president, "we will be happy to execute *your* idea—on the simple grounds that no agency can *minimize losses caused by an advertiser's damned foolishness* the way Barton, Rubicam & Belding can."

A More Subtle Difference

That story emphasizes a complex relationship. For even if the creative director of an advertising agency has a better idea than, let us say, his boss or the client, it is often his function to make a worse idea look good in order to satisfy somebody. That somebody may be anybody—from a client who thinks he knows better to a superior who *ought* to know better.

Integrity deserves to be honored, it seems to me, to the extent that the creator of the ad should try to sell his best effort. But copy chiefs are not employed primarily to be salesmen; and after one or, at the most, two good college tries, the copy chief who is a pro can honorably become a businessman, shrug his shoulders and try to make the most of a bad thing—really try, I mean. He doesn't drag his mental feet or sulk or try to sabotage (with poor copy) the campaign he has had forced on him. He doesn't try to prove he was right by doing a poor job. Nor does he stage what the psychiatrists term a "hostile surrender," submitting literally (too literally) to anything asked of him. He tries honestly to produce the best job he can, arguing every step of the way to get the effects he is after—but always within the *new and approved framework* (or "copy outline," as it is called in some shops).

I am not, of course, here arguing an abandonment of decent ethical standards. They are, in too many instances and without my urging, already abandoned. No responsible man (copy chief, account man or clerk) would lend his efforts to promoting the destinies of a product or service which he is convinced can harm the user. Nor would he apply his talents to a campaign that, in his opinion, would actually harm the sales of the product. Transgressors of these prohibitions are not, however, exactly rare. Cigarette advertising is an all too clear example of advertising harmful to the consumer. And innumerable campaigns, rushed into print to please powerful and ignorant client-officials, offer myriad examples of advertising harmful to the seller. But the difference between what an ad creator wants and what his boss or client wants is seldom so great that the issue can be decided on a basis of the harm that may possibly be done. It is almost always a more subtle difference.

The Writer—Businessman

What I am urging is simply this: that the copy chief I am using as an example must remember that he is a businessman as well as a writer. Let him remember that he can be wrong (and has been on many occasions when he set his ideas against the client's or the sales department's); and let him recognize continuously (along with his non-writing colleagues) that he is in business to make a profit. To do these things, he must know clearly and without self-deception what his advertisements are supposed to do. And one essential thing they are supposed to do is to *provide him with a livelihood.*

There are three basic rewards for success in the advertising business. One is money and all that money implies; another is the respect of your associates; and the third, which comes only after the first two have been secured, is the delicious freedom to be able to tell an advertiser or the boss to go fry his hat if he hasn't the brains to see that you are right and he is wrong. This is called "surrendering the account" or "walking out on the job." But it could also be called "indulging the successful ad man," and to reach that stage the participant must first be successful. In the process of getting that way, it is well to remember that "although not every advertisement must sell something, every ad (or almost every ad) must *satisfy the man who pays for it.*"

An Intruder in the Editorial Shrubbery

It is also well to remember this: *The man who pays for the advertisement is seldom the man who must approve it.* The men who must approve an advertisement work for the man who pays for it (the Somebody for whom every ad is prepared) and they come into daily conflict with the creator of the advertisement over two major issues. They differ with him on what is required to get the attention of readers and on how to hold that attention after it is obtained.

The sponsoring executives seem to believe, with an incredible naiveté, that merely a mention of their product will get attention; and, after that, the dear reader will go on absorbing with fascinated interest whatever information they want to feed him. On the other hand, the creator of the advertisement holds that seldom does anyone give a damn about an ad and that otherwise attentive and discriminating readers act like bird-brains and elaborately ignore gems of purest ray serene when staring glassily at the advertising pages. He believes that the reader is interested only in what he has paid for and that every ad is an intruder lurking in the editorial shrubbery hoping for a crumb of attention. He feels that it is a triumph if the ad gets its crumb and that, to do so, it must be dramatic, interruptive or unexpected, in (hopefully) good taste; and that even after attention has been obtained, every single sentence of its text must be of intense interest or the reader will wander off into the comic section or the article on the Beatles. Most of all, he wonders why those befuddled fellows who must approve the ad (to whose great advantage it would be were all these difficult objectives accomplished) make it so hard for him to accomplish them.

Do these opposing attitudes exist only because businessmen are numbskulls and advertising men are cynics? It isn't that simple. The businessman does tend to act as if he has become hypnotized by his own story and believes it so completely that he thinks everyone else will be equally fascinated. Perhaps he feels that anything in which he has invested his best attention and so much of his vital energy *must* be of interest to everyone. If so, he has certainly lost his sense of proportion.

On the other hand, the ad man has no such illusions about *his* product, the ad. He knows from bitter experience that the best he can do may well go utterly unnoticed by the reader, no matter how much effort and inventiveness he has put into it. It is no news to any ad writer that the reader cares about almost nothing except himself and that, unless he has paid to read them, the most dramatic facts about others (or their products) will leave him as aloof as the moon.

There is little doubt that these are the ad man's true convic-

tions; he gains nothing by pretending that they are if they are not. In fact, he stands to lose a great deal of respect from members of the laity who feel that he should have more faith in his product. But it may also be true that the sponsor's executives don't really believe what they profess to believe: that people are as interested in their product as they pretend to be. The whole thing may be an act—and if so, it is a disgracefully expensive one.

A Platform on Which to Posture

The truth is that the preparation and approval of advertising is a dangerously public spectacle in the upper echelons of most

businesses. Too often it is used as a platform on which an executive can stand and posture to impress his siblings and superiors.
The man who professes a fanatic's faith in his product has a
large and potentially lucrative intramural audience before which
he can perform. The ad manager impresses the vice president in
charge of marketing who impresses the president who impresses
the directors, and all are concerned with cross-impressing one another with their devotion to perfectionism in the expression of
their corporate opinions of their precious product. And it often
seems that no one is thinking about how the story will impress
the market.

The process of preparing and choosing among competing advertising campaigns and the even more arduous business of preparing each ad and submitting it to a long (much too long) list
of officials inside the sponsor's company produces a stench in the
nostrils of common sense. It tempts scores of executives and
juniors to use the opportunity to demonstrate their conscientiousness, their faith in the product, their enthusiasm for the boss' ac-
complishments, and their absorption in all sorts of details which
it is to their advantage to seem absorbed in. Human nature being
what it is, this desire to promote themselves in the opinions of
their superiors has almost always a higher priority than the desire
to promote the product more efficaciously.

The creator of the advertisement runs up against seemingly
inexplicable insistences day after day: to add this or that unim-
portant detail to the copy, to show this or that trivial feature in
the illustration, to spotlight some ancillary or irrelevant fact; and
to omit or alter what seem to him to be highly effective and exciting headlines or layout treatments. These insistences can be explained only on grounds other than a desire to improve the advertising, and the obvious explanation is that they spring from a
wish to impress superiors.

What to do about it? Only the most powerful figure at the
sponsoring organization can do anything about it at all. And here
there re-enters the picture *the man who pays for the ad,* the man
on whose desk appears the famous placard, "The Buck Stops
Here." And he probably *won't do a thing,* for the only thing he
can do is to reduce drastically the list of those who must approve
the ads, and, if he does that, he will have to do what he is paid

to do: make an intuitive judgment based largely on his experience and take the rap if he is wrong.

The Public Steps Down

In preparing advertisements for the Somebody who pays for them another great difficulty arises. You must persuade him that people seldom believe what they hear or read. It is an elementary fact of life that as we grow up all of us learn to be skeptics, cynics, or both—or we don't grow up; we stay "innocents." Gradually we learn that every group, every special interest, has its own peculiar language, an "idioglossia," as the social scientists call it. And we learn to "step down" that language or, let us say, to compensate for its exaggerations and distortions as we listen to them.

Examples abound. I guess we start this process on the bitter day we learn that mother has been fibbing when she said she loved us more than anybody else in the world. "Except," we now begin to interpolate, "that big lug, the old man."

Here's the last sentence from a long letter that I read recently in the daily newspaper: "The conclusion must be that Cranston has come to be thoroughly ashamed of its schools this summer." When I read that I said to myself, "I own a summer home here and I understand that the Cranston schools are pretty good." Then I looked at the signature and, seeing that it belonged to a "Vice President for High Schools, Cranston Teachers Guild, AFL-CIO," I stepped down the sentence at once. "The man means," I thought, "that right now, among other things, there's a shortage of teachers, money, and school buildings in Cranston."

He couldn't put it as simply as that, of course. He has to get (or sound) really outraged and excited about it, like the executives trying to impress the boss with their zeal for the product. For it is part of America's giantism, of our blind admiration of size, our dedication to continuous growth, to expect that the teacher rant unremittingly for more teachers and schools, the doctor for more doctors and hospitals, the military man for more troops and armaments. So the specialists are doing only what the rest of us idiots expect them to do—but some of them get mighty hysterical in the process, and that's one reason why the public has developed this "stepping-down" habit.

33

"Cut Out Smoking," Puffed the Doctor

And it isn't just in calling for more people like ourselves and more of our special facilities that all of us exaggerate. When your doctor tells you to cut *out* cigarettes, it is often clear from his own ash tray that he spells it "cut *down*" when he applies it to himself —and you proceed accordingly.

When your favorite sports columnist reports that the home team has "annihilated" the opposition, you take that horrendous verb with a grain of salt. "Annihilate" may mean a score anywhere from 20 to 0 all the way down to 4 to 0, depending on the state of his thyroid gland.

Even the Bible has its own level of exaggeration. Have you ever "risen from the bed of your abominations"? Don't answer, please! You know as well as I do that when the pastor lobs a phrase like that at his congregation he's referring to the quick kiss John stole from Bill's wife on the terrace last Saturday night more than to what James Branch Cabell has called "the daring, immoral and lascivious misdeeds of a desperado in sex."

What I am sneaking up on here is that the public doesn't believe what advertisements say about the products they puff any more than it believes what educators say about teaching facilities, or what doctors say about health or what columnists say about sports. In fact, the public probably doesn't believe advertisements as *much* as it believes its teachers, doctors and pastors. Because the public knows quite early in its adult life that anybody talking about anything important to him will always describe it as better and more important than it actually is.

This doubletalk has been part of our inheritance for so long that we accept it and adjust for it automatically. It has its roots in the very human need to build the ego, which says in its sly and realistic way: "Anything that I am doing must be described to *them* as vital, dynamic, essential, exciting, and thus *I* become more vital, dramatic and essential in their eyes."

Would Detroit Have Given It a Thought?

All right, so the reader adjusts as he reads (or hears) an advertisement—he *de-hyperbolizes*. But the amount of stepping down, the *degree* to which the reader corrects as he reads, is different in every category of goods and services. More than that, among widely advertised products in any category, it's different for every product. And one of the most delicate and essential jobs of the copy chief is to find the *Level of Credibility* for every product or service for which he produces copy.

When a perfume advertises *The Way to Say "Remember Me,"* the woman who buys it doesn't really think it is *the* way to make her remembered; she reads it *"a* way to say 'remember me.'"* When a home permanent wave kit states "You can look like a queen for very little jack," the girl who uses it doesn't expect to be mistaken for Elizabeth of England. When an electric shaver ad shows the backside of a naked baby and enthuses, "This will give you an idea of how your face will feel after a shave with Derma-Mower," our reaction is amusement at a good advertising idea, but no feeling of conviction that our sandpaper face is ever again going to feel like Junior's smooth rear end.

But does this mean that advertising should describe home permanent kits blandly as products that "might improve your appearance," or electric shavers as products that "give you a pretty good shave"? Not if the advertiser wants to sell them. For, as a result of years of conditioning, the market expects advertising to state its claims extravagantly, and if it doesn't, it undersells.

Advertising must say what it has to say on the Level of Credibility generally accepted for the product at hand, pitching the copy neither below nor above that level. It is as easy to make the mistake of shooting above as below—even in the perfume-permanent-electric shaver field (the field of cosmetics) where the Level of Credibility is very low indeed. Try selling a perfume as "The Secret of Brigitte Bardot's Allure" and they'll laugh you off the market! Nobody can step that one down enough to make it believable. (Bardot's got what she's got and it isn't just perfume.)

Or edit that line from Derma-Mower and the baby's backside photograph just a little. Instead of "This will give you an idea of how smooth your face will feel after a shave with Derma-Mower," make it read "This is *how* your face will feel, etc." What you get is a really incredible statement, a claim that moves over the line into a flat untruth and completely undermines the reader's faith in the product.

Booze Tells the Truth

What advertising *does* have a high Level of Credibility? Oddly enough, liquor advertising in America is so carefully regulated that almost no one doubts its truth. When an ad says, "94 Proof. Distilled from 65% Grain Neutral Spirits," we know that's what it is. When it says "Scotland's best distilleries produced this Scotch whiskey," we may raise an eyebrow a trifle at that word "best," but we do not question the rest of the line. We know it's all Scotch and all from Scotland.

And there are all sorts of Levels of Credibility in between. To demonstrate this, I conducted a small test of my own not long ago—listing on a sheet of paper five categories of products. The sheet read, simply: "Television Sets, Toothpaste, Cigarettes, Automobiles, Life Insurance," and it asked: "Without thinking too long, please put the numbers 1,2,3,4,5 next to each of the above words—the number 1 signifying that you would tend to believe the advertising of that product or service most, the number 5 signifying that you would *least* tend to believe the advertising of that product or service."

The results were astonishing, especially in view of the size of the sample. I sent out a hundred questionnaires to people in the promotion and circulation departments of a national magazine. They were clerks, typists, executives, a good cross-section, and fifty-four of them returned the questionnaires. On chance alone, there being five choices, each product could have been expected to receive 20 per cent of the votes for any position—including the highest Level of Credibility, the category whose advertising is most believed. But instead of 20 per cent, life insurance (whose advertising is heavily censored by law, like liquor's) received 70 *per cent* of all the votes for first position, the position of highest credibility.

The product with the least believable advertising and thus the lowest Level of Credibility, received more than twice as many votes as could be expected on chance alone. The winner of the cellar position was cigarettes, with 45 per cent of the votes.

At the same time I asked these respondents to rate five automobile brands in the order of their credibility. And here I got a real surprise. I had listed four different Detroit brands and Volkswagen. And there in first position was Volkswagen with a solid 80 per cent of the votes—four times as many as could be expected. The car in last position had two and a half times as many votes as could be expected, or 53 per cent. In each case, let me repeat, chance alone would account for only 20 per cent of the votes, so Volkswagen was four times as strongly established in first position as it could be expected to be, the car in the cellar two and a half times as strongly established. Were I working in Detroit, I think that I would have given this scoring a considerable amount of attention.

What do I deduce from all this? Remember that I set out to prove only that people read the advertising of different products on different Levels of Credibility. It is apparent that, although the respondents were asked to rank their reaction to *advertising,* they were actually considering also the *category images* and *brand images* that were in their minds. But if advertising doesn't help form category and brand images, what *does* advertising do? Consequently, these rankings broadly reflect the reaction of these people to the advertising, just as they were intended to do.

We can disregard the accuracy of the 80 per cent Volkswagen figure and concede that it might be 70 per cent or 60 per cent. It still shows that, for some reason, Volkswagen advertising enjoys a higher Level of Credibility than that of the other cars. People *believe* Volkswagen advertising more than they do the advertising of American cars. And even if that cigarette figure of

54 per cent is only generally accurate, it does show that people believe cigarette advertising less than (a *lot* less than) insurance advertising or even toothpaste advertising.

A Concept for Somebody

So much for the research, such as it is. Now, how do we apply this pattern of information? Here is one answer, a tentative one only. If it is indeed true that people not only expect advertising to exaggerate but they expect different products to exaggerate in different degrees (and I believe that they do), then it is the job of copy chiefs and all producers of advertising to find out *in what degree* people expect products to exaggerate. To put it differently, an individual Level of Credibility can realistically be located for every product or service advertised.

This has nothing whatsoever to do with the copy's *manner*, the wit and ingenuity of phrasing, the sparkle and originality of tone or approach or description. It has only to do with *what* is claimed in the advertising, not with *how* it is claimed. Within any given Level of Credibility, a copy chief can be as sharp or as dull as he wants to be—or can't help being.

Perhaps some day someone will be able to measure these Levels of Credibility scientifically, and then all advertising copy can be gauged on some universal scale. I doubt it, for I do not believe that the reactions of human beings can be put into this sort of mathematical table with any degree of accuracy. And I earnestly hope that no such experiment ever succeeds. It would take all the fun out of copy for those of us who produce it, and we'd all have to play second oboe to a passel of slide-rule characters. Meanwhile, I think that all producers of advertising copy ought to be aware of Levels of Credibility in the vague, half-logical, half-intuitive way in which all writers apply criteria to their work.

The Play-A-Day Writer's World

The child in all of us who write for a living knows there *is* something childlike in gravely putting words together in patterns as a way of supporting ourselves and our families. Writing, it has been said, is a peculiar process that attracts peculiar people (or it may be that the act of writing tends to make its practitioners that way). And one way in which writers are peculiar was expressed years ago by the same Mr. Cabell I quoted earlier. Said he with great simplicity in his book on writing, *Beyond Life*, "The literary artist labors primarily to divert himself."

I am not claiming that a copy man trying to turn out a trade ad on steel I-beams for, let us say, *Iron Age* is a literary artist—although he may be. But there is a difference of a very basic kind between the way he earns his salary and the way a financier, salesman, engineer, manufacturer, clerk, or anyone else provides for himself. He is, as Cabell says, probably diverting himself. If you

press him hard enough he will even admit that there is an element of play in his work—a kind of childish fun, without which, incidentally, he tends to be a lousy writer.

The Bible says that a man should earn his bread "in the sweat of his face," and I have always felt that what the Bible means is that a man ought not to enjoy himself too much when he is working. This is probably a Calvinist interpretation, and I am no Calvinist. Nevertheless, I've always enjoyed writing and editing so much that it has left me feeling a bit guilty. In some manner, somehow, I seem to feel that I've been getting away with something all my working life. Maybe those of us who feel this way ought to keep this thing more of a secret.

At any rate, the Level of Credibility is offered here as a new technique in anything but a spirit of fun. Quite the contrary, it is a serious attempt to find a new method of weighing the effectiveness of advertising's communication with its audiences. Certainly it is a concept most desirable to make clear to that *Somebody* who is paying for the advertising.

Ventilating the Pockets of Silence

There is one more point which, in fairness to that Somebody, should be set down here. It deals with the miles of advertising copy written solely for the education of the client. Ads like these have been written since the dawn of the ad business, and they will continue to be written until the last typewriter is stilled. You might imagine an unusual *Somebody,* addressing the following letter to his ad agency:

Personal and Confidential

Dear Bob:

Now that our contract for the year is signed and sealed, I thought you might like to know the real reason why our account went to your agency again instead of to any one of four other agencies who were after our business.

It was because of all the stuff you've done for us that never got approved.

Your agency must be filled with people who, whenever our name is mentioned, snap right back with, "Why the hell don't they make up

their minds what they want over there?" Well, the answer is: (a) that we didn't know how much disagreement there was among our top management until you started to put our advertising story together and (b) that you have helped us make up our minds about so many things during the past year that perhaps there will be less reason for people to ask that question next year.

These last twelve months have been a revelation to me. I am astonished and disturbed to realize that intelligent, realistic men can live in such a fool's paradise. Most of my chief executives and I have worked together for years, believing all the time that we held the same basic views about our business, while, in fact, we differed gravely on important policies and issues. I guess what happened was that there were always great areas of general agreement among us, within which we could discuss matters amicably and constructively. Each time the talk wandered out of those areas, we steered it back to prevent bickering, open disagreement, and even serious quarreling. But over the years this business of "getting along together" produced pockets of silence on subjects of great importance to our company. The longer each of these pockets was left unventilated, the more emotionally identified with it became the member of management whose special, unshared point of view it represented.

The decision to advertise more of Consolidated's products more vigorously was what brought our account to you in 1964. That decision also made it necessary for us to open up those pockets of silence all through our business. Consequently, almost every ad or commercial you showed us seemed to precipitate conflict among two or three of us—conflict which, in at least half the cases, never *was* resolved and which finally killed the ad or commercial under discussion. You would show copy to Bill; he would finally get it right as he saw it; he would send it on to me and I would be astonished to learn that this was the opinion of my executive vice president on how that particular product ought to be sold. Or the division heads would approve something, submit it to Bill, and he would be similarly outraged. And often, when they brought the matter to me for a decision, I found I disagreed with them both.

As you know, this dissension among us caused copy to be written again and again before we found the right way to say things (which means "before we could agree among ourselves"). But, meanwhile, *what an invaluable service you were performing for us!* If all those type-written pages of copy and planning that you submitted and revised and re-revised so patiently had been bound into a book, it would tell a fascinating story of misunderstandings slowly and painfully being welded into agreement. And it would also, as I said, constitute a major exhibit in any presentation explaining why you continue to handle our account (for, I cannot resist adding, the very handsome new fee, plus commissions).

I wonder why more advertising agencies don't let writers and thinkers know that their business is not merely to produce good ads. Perhaps it is even more important for them to get in there with their typewriters and help client managements face up to their intramural misunderstandings.

It's a noble service, and I wanted to express our deep gratitude for the way you have rendered it.

My best to Joe T. and to Roy. It ought to be a great year for arguing!

Cordially,
Oscar de Gotha, President
Consolidated Products, Inc.

There's a Somebody for you! Mr. Oscar de Gotha, I know a hundred creative advertising men who would work their brain-cells into scrapple to be put on your account. May Consolidated Products prosper and your rule be long!

"They send those engineers out from Toronto to ask me if I think the road ought to change over from steam to oil. Are they crazy? Here I've spent forty years learning how to run a steam-powered railroad and they ask me a question like that!"
—REMARK ATTRIBUTED TO THE WESTERN MANAGER OF THE UNION PACIFIC RAILROAD, CIRCA 1935.

DELUSION III

"The agency puts your money where it will do you the most good"

*Most of the statements in this chapter apply to
only about 95 per cent of the companies advertising today and to only about 98 per cent of the
agencies. They are irrelevancies in the case of the
very few multimillion-dollar accounts and the still
fewer very large agencies serving them. All others:*
"Attention, please!"

THE ADVERTISING AGENCY system has been criticized for many
things but seldom do we hear the case stated against its chief absurdity. Only the very largest advertisers seem to realize that an
agency cannot be expected to be both the judge and the jury; it
cannot be expected to analyze the clients' needs and then pre-
scribe for them objectively as if it were not itself a business with a
profit motive. Seldom does anyone make the point that, like any
other business, an agency should not be expected to recommend
products it does not make nor services that its competitors render
more efficiently, more brilliantly or more economically. To expect
it to suggest that its clients use advertising techniques in which it
does not excel is to expect the oil burner salesman to recommend
gas or electric heat.

Nor is it often observed that advertising has become so complex and its specialties so numerous that only a handful of the
very largest agencies are in a position to face a marketing problem with an open mind—favoring no single technique over any
other. The agency with only a vestigial sales promotion department is not prepared (or inclined) to recommend that a large part
of its client's appropriation be spent in direct mail; and the agency
whose greatest strength is in television will hardly tend to suggest
that large sums be spent on posters and exhibits in airports, ter-
minals and other transportation media or that 75 per cent of the
client's ad dollars go into newspapers or magazines.

44

To See How Ad Men Misbehave, Ponder the Case of Burma-Shave

Several decades ago the people who make Burma-Shave were ready to go out of business when one of the owners thought up the boards with the serialized doggerel that were to become part of the country's folklore. The first series (unrhymed) were tried out on a few roads leading into a not very metropolitan Midwest metropolis and the results were apparent at once. The following year and every year thereafter more and more money was put into the signs while Burma-Shave sales burgeoned. The appropriation was at one time a very large one, a plum for any agency.

But what agency today, would have kept almost 100 per cent of an advertising budget that size in a gimmick not even dreamed up by an ad man? Whatever agencies handled Burma-Shave during the years of its growth must have put increasing pressure on the client to divert at least some of his funds into more conventional channels. Agencies with strong radio departments must have snowed him with arguments calculated to pull him out of the roadside ditches and up on the airwaves. Agencies especially strong on design must have tempted him with alluring artwork, urging him constantly to replace his jingles with twenty-four-sheet posters or full-color reproductions in the magazines. It must have been only the happy, triple-barreled fact that the owner thought up the signs in the first place, that he retained faith in his own idea and that he continued to control the purse strings that kept his money concentrated where it would do him the most good.*

* Just before this volume went to press the Burma-Shave jingle reappeared in, of all places, television. In the commercial, a road appears on a split screen whose other half shows the comely oriental face of what must be a Burma maiden. The road slips away as if seen through the windshield of a car; the signs appear one by one (*"Within this vale / Of toil and sin / Your head grows bald / But not your chin! / BURMA-SHAVE."*)—and the Burmese maiden speaks them as they slip by. But why? Wouldn't Burma-Shave have done better to have stayed on the roads and highways where it was a beloved king of its medium rather than try to shoe-horn its way into costly, crowded television where it takes a fortune like the Moulmein Pagoda to make any impression at all? But that's Agency-Biz for you!

The Blessed Single Versus the Accursed Multiple

There is another front that must be watched with never-flagging vigilance if an advertiser wants to make sure that his money is put where it will yield the best and fastest results. In trying to produce advertisements, commercials, direct mail, every agency has a tendency to aim for *The Single Solution,* one that lends itself to a single appeal that can appear everywhere in almost the same form and produce agency commissions every time it shows up. (The round-headed little figures, half goops and half kewpies, used in Campbell's Soups' advertising are a perfect example.) This contrasts with *The Multiple Solution,* abhorred by every agency because it requires special creative work and production of different themes especially adapted to the different media in which they appear: often a score of magazines, newspapers, stations and channels.

The single idea is always seductive; everyone wishes he could hit upon and stick with "Ask the Man Who Owns One" or "Time to Re-Tire" or "Good to the Last Drop." I name these three ancient but excellent single-idea themes because they have gone the way of all themes, into limbo. Perhaps they shouldn't have. Perhaps they were dropped merely because new ad directors or new agencies couldn't stand agreeing that themes invented by predecessors were still good enough to continue appearing. And so away they went—and maybe their murderers were right. For even a fine campaign idea will sooner or later make an audience yawn—and just when is anybody's educated guess.

Some control over this universal phenomenon can be obtained by instituting a program of continuing research to signal the moment when the idea begins to pall. But to do this kind of job as it should be done is painfully expensive—and therefore impractical for all but the largest advertisers. This is just another way in which the giants manage to keep several jumps ahead of the monster, monotony, while their smaller competitors are boring their markets into slumber.

Someone once said that the first man to compare a woman to a rose was a genius while the last one was an ass. And just as that fragrant simile passed its peak some while back and has had an increasingly sour flavor ever since, many "great campaign ideas" (like the Green Giant, of whom I am terribly, terribly tired) keep

appearing long after people have started muttering, "Oh, Gawd!"

To anticipate critics of this attack on superannuated campaigns, let me put things in perspective. A few good ideas (like "The Pause that Refreshes" and "You Can Be Sure If It's Westinghouse") bear repeating for a long time. Some ideas of this magnitude are admittedly abandoned by impatient or unappreciative managements long before they deserve to be. But that sin is infrequent and trivial compared to the huge and heinous crime that permits thousands of bad ideas to be repeated over and over until reels the mind and rises the gorge because the agencies involved are too lazy (or too resolved to save creative salary and time) to dream up new and better campaigns.

The ideal advertisement from almost any agency's point of view is one that can be prepared just once and then be published over and over again in a long list of media without the investment of additional creative or production time and talent. If, a few months later, the ad can run again in as large or larger a list with, perhaps, just a small change of copy, the agency treasurer is likely to recommend that the employee who thought up the coup get a dandy raise. To further this understandable economic objective agencies will argue loudly and forever that it is so hard to get "one really good ad" that, once you've got one, it is only good sense to print it in all publications where it can do you any good, regardless of their dissimilarity. They also claim that the one good commercial is equally rare and ought to be broadcast on stations from New York's Westchester County to the parishes of Louisiana. There are two things wrong with these statements. Good ads aren't that hard to do—and any ad that is the best possible ad for the readers of *Life* cannot possibly also be the best possible ad for the readers of the *National Geographic Magazine*. The same ad may be *effective* in both magazines; no one denies that. But one ad cannot be the most effective advertisement it is possible to produce for any two publications with different audience characteristics.

All Audiences Are Different

And all magazines claim that their audiences are different from those of all other magazines. Returning to that *Life* and *National Geographic* combination, it is true that some people read both of these books. But the great majority of *Life's* readers do not read *Geographic* and a very large percentage of *Geographic's* readers do not read *Life*. Even a casual glance at the audience statistics shows that an ad for *Life* must be pitched more broadly and to a lower incomed, less educated group than one written for *National Geographic*—or for *The New Yorker, Harper's, Atlantic, Time, U.S. News, Fortune* and many others.

In the best of all possible ad worlds—one in which every dollar was being spent with complete, knowledgeable conscientiousness—there would be a different ad written for almost every one of the more than twenty magazines that appear on the lists of many medium-sized advertisers who take columns and half columns in all sorts of publications. But this is almost never done—and the reasons why are inadequate. The talent is available if agencies want to pay for it and run the risk of seeing some bright people run off with some of their accounts occasionally. The truly confident agency allows for this (a few do) and plans for attrition as the price of attracting new and demanding clients.

We see some mighty astonishing examples of how campaigns are stretched to cover the strangest bedfellows. This is especially visible in the advertising of public utilities and companies given to "image-building." Where no result will be visible or palpable from the advertising for many years, the tendency is to prepare *"a nice campaign showing nice people saying nice things about our good company."* (An actual quote from an internal memorandum.) All this niceness results in a kind of unremarkable respectability which, in turn, helps to produce what is probably the greatest, most expensive and beautifully engraved collection of unread advertisements in the world: the so-called "institutional" advertisements of America's great corporations. Sometimes *Playboy* will get the same bland copy as *Good Housekeeping,* as if there were no boys and no girls—only neuters to pour warm milk over. Often the same ad will appear in *Seventeen* and *Argosy.* It seems to me that the least we should expect is one ad for the shelter magazines (*Better Homes and Gardens* and *House Beautiful*), a different one for the women's magazines (*Good Housekeeping, McCall's, Woman's Day*), a different one again for the mass magazines (*Life, Look, Reader's Digest*), a still different one for the upper middlebrows (*The New Yorker, Atlantic, Harper's, Saturday Review*), and another variant for the news magazines (*Time, U.S. News, Newsweek*).

Who Will Ride the Wild Mustang?

Considering the naughty tendency of any agency to recommend to its clients only those services it performs most effectively and to do things for its own profit first, one would think (wouldn't one?) that the advertiser would employ a strong and knowledgeable ad man as his ad director. How else can management know it is selecting the right agency for each stage of its development; how else can it ride herd on its agency product group and get its money's worth; how else can it pick the right moment to switch agencies, the moment when its growth or diminishment or change of marketing problems indicates that a different pattern of agency services is required? But, except in the biggest advertiser companies, the ad director tends to be weak, unsavvy and without respect even in his own company.

The reasons for this illogicality shift and slide around so much —they are so unconvincing as they are discussed endlessly at various meetings of ad managers around the country—that one suspects there is some half-ashamed human weakness behind them. As indeed there is. Sometimes it is the weakness of a president who, knowing he knows nothing about advertising, still wants to have his say about it and be the last word on the subject inside his company anyway. (Just as everybody thinks he can write, so does every businessman think he has the genius of the Burma-Shave proprietor who jingled his way to riches.) Or perhaps it isn't the president who holds down the status of the ad manager in his company, but the vice president in charge of sales.

"Good advertising is only good selling!" is a cliché that has produced more bad advertising (and worse ad managers) than any other six words in the language!

Yet sales managers are notoriously persuasive gents and the continuous iteration of this senseless saw in prexy's ear often helps the sales manager get the ad manager put on his staff. Once there, under the sales department's thumb, he is prevented from producing any advertising except hard-sell stuff and sales aids.

Finally, of course, come the simple mathematics supposed to clinch the matter. It is nonsense, says someone, to pay an ad manager $25,000 a year to administer a $150,000 advertising appropriation. "That's almost 15 per cent of the whole business!" he observes, thus showing his aptitude for mental arithmetic if for little else. For of course 20 per cent or even 40 per cent in some cases, is not too much to pay to see that a larger sum is intelligently administered. One pays what one must; there are only a few good men and they come high, if they come at all. Many intelligent creative people can find more satisfying ways to make a living than to grow ulcers as an advertising director. As Jack Neuman put it recently, speaking of his own successful career in television, "I'm sick of the business. Maybe I'm nuts, but I think that the industry should do something more than just stand around and look stupid." (New York *Times,* April 4, 1965). In the long run, the ad director who wants to hold his job must often do just that. Caught between the agency and his boss, passed over and around, all he can do is stand there glumly and look stupid.

"Pick Your Master, Man!"

One of the more amusing and less edifying spectacles in the business world is to watch an advertiser (not, as I said, a multi-million-dollar advertiser; they know better) go about the delicate business of hiring a new ad director *with the help of the agency.* The last six words are italicized to emphasize the incredible hypocrisy and stupidity of the proceeding.

For just what *is* the ideal ad director from the agency's point of view? He is a man who will let the agency have its own way in everything while giving his employer the impression that he is the dedicated steward, the loyal guardian of the royal exchequer. The less he knows about advertising the better the agency likes it and so the agency principals do their best to persuade the client that, "You don't need an ad man so much as a good liaison man—a capable executive who can mesh our facilities with yours, get our ads and commercials before the proper people fast for their approval on time, so we can keep our schedules with a minimum of overtime and delay. He should be able to interpret our needs to you and your needs to us skillfully and sensitively, but he doesn't need to have any real opinions of his own."

Frank as that statement seems—it is made in those very words in many cases—many other things are left unsaid. For example: "We're the advertising experts around here and you don't need anyone else to tell you (or certainly us) what is and is not good advertising. Don't put a man in there who is so ambitious or so strong that he can stand between your top management and us. We want access to your top people at all times—how else can we keep you sold and smell the first signs that you're getting restless for a new connection? And, above all, don't give this fellow the right to hire or even suggest a new agency. That's too important a job for you to delegate." The whole idea of having an advertising director at all is to add an informed ad man to top management and then delegate advertising to him, but try telling that to your agency.

In simple fact there is no good reason why a firm should not have several agencies if it has an advertising director strong enough to handle them—and some very successful companies have: one agency for television, let us say, one for print media, another for sales promotion, another for foreign advertising and promotion. The competition among them can work out to the great advantage of the client. But the agencies won't like it. They'll growl and mutter and use their claws. It takes a darned good man with a long whip and a sturdy kitchen chair to handle all those lions in one ring.

How to Knife an Ad Director

The ad agency will do all it can to get the strong ad director into trouble.

Its executives will knock him to his bosses; they'll short-circuit him; they'll sabotage his ideas. They'll deliberately assign their worst people to him and blame the bad work on his inability to "communicate," they'll itemize his extravagances or financial mistakes to the firm's treasurer and his extramarital adventures to the stuffiest director on the board—and, if they get him fired, they'll alert all the other agencies to keep him out of a decent job if they can. But the big advertisers come in here. *Their best source of talent* (and they well know it) *is the ad director abhorred by the agencies.*

The agencies will, in brief, do everything short of losing the account to shake this kind of rider off their backs. And not even short of that, for the record is studded with agencies who have "surrendered" accounts rather than be checked up on by a capa-

ble, firm and vigilant ad director. Why *should* they put up with this sort of thing (unless there are huge commissions) when so many of their clients will let them help select the ad manager and keep his salary and status so low that he has no power.

Sad to say, most managements won't go through the difficult and painful business of first finding and then paying for a good man in this job. The agency principals are so persuasive, so pleasant to be with, so seemingly logical. The candidates for the advertising managership often seem to be unpleasantly smooth smart-alecks, extremely unsubservient. Often they act superior because they know what they know—and that management knows little or nothing about their specialty, while other firms are bidding for them.

Pity the Poor Prexy

Sometimes I find myself being sorry for managements with a really strong ad director. The arrogant so-and-so, when he knows his own strength, will manipulate his management and his agencies as if they both worked for *him*. He'll tempt his management with advertising, promotion and publicity ideas so good, that, time and again, they'll authorize appropriations beyond his budget—and he'll keep his agencies in a ferment trying to execute his ideas to his satisfaction. The top ad director knows that tempo is everything—and he never stops pushing new ideas and demands at both his bosses and his agencies. He gets way with this as long as he produces, but the moment he nods—Bop!

Off with his head! It's a dangerous life but an exciting one and some men seem to be able to make it a long one. Meanwhile the president and other officials will do well to practice forebearance and count themselves fortunate in having advertising that sparkles plenty and sales curves that climb under its brilliance.

The Non-Ad Non-Director

Of course, not all ad directors have that title. Often the managers of the divisions or the president or the executive vice-president runs the ad show and has an ad director just to indicate that he knows how to delegate (which he obviously doesn't). The character on top may or may not be an advertising man, willing or unwilling to spend the time and effort needed to get the best results out of his ad appropriation. If he's a tyro at advertising or buried in other matters, you can be sure that his sit-in can do little to prevent the agency from doing what it wants while Mr. Big is off whoring after new plants or new customers. Inevitably, when Mr. Big gets back, the agency has done something he doesn't like, undeterred by the frantic cries of his figurehead ad manager. In which case he chews out (or throws out) the ad manager. It doesn't matter which. That kind of guy is a dime a dozen anyway.

At his worst, he is indeed a pitiful figure, knowing little about advertising and nothing about managing. He is the clerk in charge of the firm's mailing lists; he checks the agency's bills; he buys the firm's printed matter but only after getting three estimates and showing them to his superior; a junior account executive at the agency takes him out and buys him a free lunch and a few drinks once a month, and every Christmas the agency's president sends him a poinsettia and a form letter beginning, "I want to take this opportunity to say how pleasant it has been to work with you this year—" It certainly has. Like a perfect waiter, the guy has been almost invisible.

If we think of advertisers as if they were members of the United Nations Assembly (a body in which the United States and

Chad have each one vote), then it is probably true that some-where between 75 per cent and 80 per cent of all advertising managers are like the miserable specimen I have just described. And thus will it be evermore—for it is not in the cards to expect the top management of small- and medium-appropriation ad-vertisers either to hire good men for those jobs or to learn any-thing much about advertising themselves.

It's just one of those slovenly facts that feed a major generaliza-tion about business and all the activites of mankind. Man is part of nature and nature is profligately wasteful. Millions of fish are hatched so that thousands may live. Billions of seeds are scat-tered to produce a few clumps of blue gentians. And most com-panies that prosper do so only because their wastefulness and in-efficiencies are less than those of their competitors. A great majority of all new businesses fail—and seldom because their advertising money is wasted. Management makes much bigger booboos than this. Let's keep our sense of proportion.

"Wait a minute!" said the Devil. "I've surveyed those other universes and only 11.9 per cent want a new solar system created. In fact 42.3 per cent said they would go somewhere else if you persist in this Garden of Eden stuff and—"
"Go away," said the Lord. "I'm busy."

DELUSION IV

"Too much attention is being paid to creativity and not enough to marketing"

"Let's take Elmer off the Spasmo account. We've impressed the client long enough, and we need real creative talent to get some new business."

No agency will keep its best creative people on an account any longer than it has to. We can go further than this: every agency tends constantly to downgrade the quality of the creative personnel it has assigned to any account that permits it to do so. The price of good creative talent is eternal client vigilance.

Thus, although the brilliant principal of Genius and Drab, Inc., may work on your account long enough to obtain it and get a theme established, he turns the whole thing over to his vice president and creative director (of which there is only one in his shop) as soon as things start moving. Two months later the creative director passes control along to a creative supervisor (of which there are six in the shop) and two months after that a senior copywriter is supervising the creation of ads and commercials for you (there are fourteen senior copywriters in the shop). If you don't stay awake and aggressive, you will find before the year is out that the top creative man on your account is a ten-thousand-dollar copywriter (of which there are thirty-seven in the agency).

This tendency of creative direction to run downhill is one of the universal laws of agency procedure; I know of no exceptions. Now that the fee system is taking the place of the commission system, things are a little (but only a very little) better. Theoretically when you pay a fee, you get what you pay for. If you want a better creative man, you pay a higher fee and one is supposed to appear. But there are two reasons why this isn't so—and both reasons apply even more forcefully where an agency operates on the commission system.

The reasons are: (a) There is a disastrous shortage of good creative men who are willing to put up with the damn foolishness that working for an agency involves and (b) George Genius and his partner, Drab, are scared to death that a good creative man will team up with a good account executive and walk off with the business to start an agency of their own.

One, Two, Three—SHIFT!

The agency's need to keep shifting its few creative stars is obvious. It wants to attract new business and it needs creative thinking to do so; current accounts are always being stalked by competitors and the creative men must be thrown into the breach to ward off losses; a very few savvy accounts keep up an unrelenting pressure to hold the best men in the agency or to get even better ones and they must be appeased or be abandoned to the competition. This condition has spawned a bunch of misstatements and outright lies calculated to sedate the restless client and make third rate creative work look good. Some of them are:

1) *The Campaign Dodge.* It is very useful for an agency to persuade a client that a good idea must be iterated and reiterated *ad nauseam* for maximum sales impact. This makes it possible for George Genius and his creative director to produce one good ad—and assign a long line of pitiful $10,000-a-year mediocrities to the job of producing endless (and largely uninspired) variations of it.

Meanwhile George and the c.d. can move on to put out other fires or blow on other embers. It is, of course, perfectly true that a good advertising idea bears repeating—that it must, indeed, be repeated often before it is even noticed by the market. It is equally true, however, that it takes just as much creative dexedrine to produce really good variations on a theme as it did to get up the original—and that even the greatest ad idea runs down after a rather limited number of variations. By somewhere near the sixth ad in the series the reader glances at the layout or headline, says to himself, "I've seen *that* before!" and turns the page.

2) *Talent Escalation.* The canny advertiser would do well to glower and look with harsh suspicion upon any attempt to change his creative horse in midstream. A skillful account man can sell his agency's packhorse art directors and hack writers with such persuasiveness that, unless the advertiser has the sales resistance of a eunuch to Pussy Galore, he will find himself falling for the buildup of "our Horace Grunt" before the fourth lunch on the subject at *The Four Seasons.* At the fifth lunch he meets Horace who has, if little else, the ability to keep his mouth shut and look creative while he is described as George Genius' heir apparent. Only after a year of cold-fish copy served up on square layouts does the client find that Horace has been bounced off three other accounts and that he is Grunt's Last Stand.

3) *Your Own Team.* This is one of the most seductive methods of palming off tyros on an account that deserves and requires pros. The pitch goes like this:

Agency Man: You know you have your choice, Bob, of keeping Hal Sturgiss or finding someone at the shop you can train in your own way of doing things. Hal's great, but he's had so much experience that he's a little inflexible and—uh—cynical. A younger guy who could get religion might be a good idea.

Advertiser: Sturgiss is OK with me. He's doing a great job.

Agency Man: Sure he is; he always does until he gets bored. Not that he'll bore easy working with *you*, Bob, with your ability to inspire people. He'll probably set a record for staying interested. But he's rather, shall we say "jaded"—and he's too valuable to force into a mold. When he asks for out, we'll have to shift him. Now a guy like Colin Gates who has no very deeply ingrained habits and is bushy-tailed and eager can stay with you and Continental for years and years and be your boy all the way. . . .

It takes a very strong man indeed to hold out for Sturgiss under a barrage like that. Especially since George Genius is instructing Sturgiss to "get bored and restless, Hal" at another restaurant during the very luncheon when the subject is broached. Which brings us to the next bit of manipulation:

4) *The Indispensable Man*. Behind a very great many incidents that occur during the course of an agency's relations with any given account is a primary realization on the part of the agency principal or principals. It is of first importance, all agree, to convince the client that, although the agency offers a great plethora of services, the essential ingredient is the proprietor, owner and president, George Genius (or some other solidly imprisoned member of the management). For example, one very famous ad agency prexy is famous for deliberately assigning to his accounts teams of creative and service executives who hate each other's guts. It is only a matter of time, he knows before the account will be all snarled up and give him an opportunity to walk in and untangle the Gordian knot with a few deft twists of his brain (and authority). After it's all over, he doesn't even have to say, "See? If it wasn't for old George Genius, where would you be?" The words hang in the air unspoken but audible to all. Outside agencies gunning for the account are often rendered impotent by such tactics.

5) *People-Reaching*. Another and most important technique for undermining a client's impatient insistence on sharp, effective creative ideas is to keep talking "Thousands of people reached per dollar." In every area of media analysis, the Nose Counters

are out in force. Prodded by the agency's media department and its computers, top management at the advertiser's offices is forever judging the worth of advertising by *how many people it is reaching* for its money. The only intelligent measurement, however, is *how many people are being involved* for the money. There is an important difference here. In magazine advertising, for instance, client management invariably thinks of the value of its advertising in terms of how many copies of its advertisement the magazine can deliver to the prospect for how much. Thus, if it spends a thousand dollars and 100,000 magazines containing its ad are distributed, it says to itself: "This ad costs me a cent a prospect."

That may be true, but it is still nonsense. Any advertising man worth his profit sharing will announce at this juncture that the people who *don't read your ad don't do anything for you.* It's as if you never got that part of the magazine's circulation. The only sense-making calculation is to figure your cost on the number of people who *read* what you have written. If you do that, however, you arrive at a new and not-so-popular arithmetic. It goes like this: 100,000 advertisements are distributed for a thousand dollars. Of these, say 20,000 are read—at least in part—and that's pretty good. Now the cost is not one cent but five cents each—a far more realistic price. But it's not a figure top management likes. The comptroller may, in fact, blow a fuse when he hears it for the first time and compares it with his old-fashioned figures.

The cost of every advertisement ought to be figured in *three* ways. The first is total cost. The second is cost-per-unit-of-advertising-distributed. But that cost is meaningless unless quoted alongside the cost-per-unit-read. To ignore this third cost is to waste the stockholders' money. For it is largely by concentrating on the cost-per-unit-perceived that management can save money on its advertising.

In a recent issue of the *Harvard Business Review,* Daniel Yankelovich, president of the Daniel Yankelovich Research organization, reported on a method of "segmenting markets." A major aim of such segmentation, he said, is to make sure that the people to whom you are about to advertise are not already so sold on a competing product, or so prejudiced against using any product of the kind you are selling, that *no amount* of advertising can possibly win them as customers. For my purpose here, exposures to such people cannot be counted as perceived *no matter how thoroughly the advertisements are read.*

For what doth it profit the advertiser of a man's deodorant to reach hundreds of thousands of men who feel it is masculine to smell of sweat and feminine to "dab stuff under yer arm"? The readership of certain newspapers and magazines, the audiences of certain radio and TV stations, are fragrant with such men.

Only recently has it been understood that the population problem of many of the world's underprivileged countries will almost certainly not (repeat *not*) be solved by making any number of absolutely efficient contraceptive pills available to their women. Why? Because of something the Latins term *machismo*, or manliness. If a man is so poor that he can't show any possessions except children, then his best way of proving he is more of a man than his next-door pauper is to have more children than he has. Consequently, if his wife does not produce a child for him every year, out she goes on her pudenda and a better bearer moves in. Is it any wonder that the experiments don't work under these circumstances? Would any amount of advertising "sell" these pills under such conditions?

$7.70 *For a Thousand Readers; or* $20.55?

Let us for a moment, however, forget these more subtle ways of wasting advertising money. Let us illustrate our point with an advertisement many people will remember: the renowned Volkswagen ad, headlined "Think Small." Everybody, including Starch, agreed that it was one of the most widely read and noted ads of the year. In *Sports Illustrated* that ad cost (on the one-time basis) exactly $6,160. Dividing that number by the page rate of *Sports Illustrated's* primary audience (2,200,000) produces the cost-per-unit-distributed, about ¼¢ each. But this represents merely the cost of having the advertisement put into the hands of 2,200,000 people in an 84-page magazine with 32 pages of competing advertisements. Nobody knows whether those people read that advertisement or not, only that it was distributed to them. And that the distribution cost ¼¢ each.

Nobody believes that any single advertisement in a magazine containing other ads is read by all of the people who buy the issue. How many people, then, could have been expected to read the Volkswagen ad in *Sports Illustrated*—the best-read single black and white page in the issue? The answer is about 800,000. And there is the ad's real cost. For if 1,400,000 of *Sports Illustrated*'s readers do not read your ad, you have no reason to figure them in your cost accounting. Thus your cost-per-unit of advertising *perceived* is 800,000 divided into the page cost ($6,160), or ¾¢ per unit. And that is three times the cost-per-unit-distributed.

It is still a fantastically low cost. On another page of the issue appears what must be termed (unfortunately) an average automobile advertisement. Instead of a challenging headline like "Think Small," its caption reads, "Upmobile Superiority." The advertiser goes on from that high peak of interest to talk admiringly about himself. But how many of *Sports Illustrated*'s readers are listening? Generosity produces a figure of some 300,000— most of whom, it seems to me, must either have been compulsive readers or students engaged in research on ipsolalia (a morbid condition in which the patient keeps talking to himself).

Thus, of two ads of the same size in the same issue of the same magazine, one secured readers for ¾¢ each, the other had to pay almost three times as much, or more than two cents each. In terms of rate-per-page-per-thousand, Volkswagen paid only $7.70 to get a thousand readers of its ad; Upmobile had to pay $20.55.

The Chairman Wanted a Feeling

Beyond establishing the real cost of advertising (cost-per-unit-perceived), the salutary lesson above reveals the ability of a good headline or a striking piece of art work to *reduce advertising's cost-per-unit-perceived*.

It is true that art work can sometimes be more expensive than it has to be, and that hiring a Joseph Heller to write the copy for a department store billing-insert can be impractical. Yet, there is relatively little over-hiring of creative talent in the advertising business today and absurdly much making-do and trading down. Agencies and services are fired because their habits of buying good art and good copy are too costly. Or their fees are too high —often because they have some expensive (i.e. creatively effective) brains on the staff.

The businessmen who pay advertising's bills do not seem to realize this fact: *every time they tolerate inferior brains, or less effective layout and artwork, they reduce the number of people likely to read and heed their message.* Thus they are throwing away more and more of their money on *distributed but unread* advertising. The object of any advertisement is to get itself read. All the research and copywriting, all the typography, story boarding, brainstorming, is effort and money down the drain unless *the ad gets read.* And most ads or commercials do not get read or heard—they are not *perceived.*

Here, for example, is a familiar situation. A drug house wants to tell America's physicians about its new tranquilizer. But it's the end of the budget cycle in the ad department and they are short of money. They can spend, say, only 60 per cent of what they need to do the kind of thorough job they usually do. What happens? In almost all such cases they "make-do." They get out a substandard mailing to their full list. Their price-per-unit-distributed is low, but almost no one reads the mailing and their price-per-unit-perceived is astronomical.

Occasionally, though, I am happy to record—and more often than in the past—an ad department confronted with this situation takes what money it has left and turns out a really effective job, covering, perhaps, only half its mailing list.

Why is this sensible procedure (obviously the result of painfully unrewarding past efforts) not adopted more widely in the business world? The answer, as usual, reposes in the vast twilight world of "human nature." Human nature can be described as those qualities in others that one most despises in himself, and all of us are guilty of blaming our errors on it. In the case of the new tranquilizer, it is human nature to give the company chairman or president what he wants—and what he wants is *the feeling that the company has announced its new drug to the entire medical profession.* But in this and all similar cases, it is only a *feeling* that top management gets; there is no substance behind it. The drug has *not* been announced—except to the printer.

The wonder is that top management so seldom sees through this little conspiracy. Somewhere, somehow, it should have acquired the savvy to realize that covering a company's entire list with a cheap or undistinguished mailing is as plain a waste of money as putting a bad ad in a magazine going to millions of excellent prospects.

And somehow, somewhere, client management should also have faced up to a big, unpleasant fact hovering over the entire

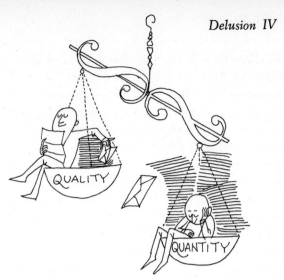

area of cost accounting in advertising. The truth is that it is relatively easy to figure all the costs mentioned above except the most important one: the cost-per-advertising-unit-perceived. The total cost, cost-per-unit-distributed, cost-per-order-sold, are easy mathematical calculations. *But how do you find out how many people read an advertising message but do not act on it?*

Good Money Cast Before Bad

There are ways. Everyone concerned knows about the Starch surveys, the Sindlinger reports, and others—not perfect, certainly, but indicative. And other, more direct studies have been made to supplement them—notably among the recipients of the direct mail sent out by the American Heritage Publishing Company, the Book-of-the-Month Club, Time, Inc., and the Ford Motor Company. The stories they tell differ in detail but are remarkably alike in their general conclusions: originality of approach, freshness of phrasing, color and art, good printing, first-class letter-shop work—each builds up the readership and lowers the cost-per-unit-perceived.

The New York *Times* is offering a service to advertisers willing to contract for a certain minimum amount of space. Its plan is almost the prototype of the sensible, civilized approach to this problem. The service will be in four parts. Part I will survey a cross-section of the *Times'* audience to discover what it already knows about the company or product that plans to advertise. From this survey will emerge Part II of the service, involving the preparation of test advertisements based on the information uncovered. Part III will test the effectiveness of the advertisements in advance of publication on a cross-section of the *Times'* readership to determine which are the most effective appeals. Part IV, a survey made after the advertising campaign has been published, will measure the changes that have occurred in the minds of the audience as a result of the appearance of the ads.

Needless to say, this is an expensive procedure and the costs of the various surveys, which require personal interviews by trained people and the careful organization of truly representative samples, will have to be shared by the publication and the advertiser. The question is: how many advertisers will be willing to meet their share of these costs? Certainly it is true that management has invariably shown a regrettable reluctance to spend money to make sure that it isn't wasting money. The trouble with expenditures like this (from the viewpoint of myopic managements) is that you have nothing to show for your research money. If the ads work, your critics will say that they would have worked anyway; that it was the product that sold on its merits, or the copy, or the art work, or the medium in which the ads appeared, or that the lucky break of their appearance at just the right time was responsible. If the ads fail, the research money was good money cast before bad.

It is not necessary to research every mailing or advertising campaign to profit from the broad body of knowledge already collected on the subject. It is necessary only to know, remember, and apply the knowledge already acquired. And the essence of that knowledge is: Only the units of advertising *perceived* are of any significance in measuring advertising costs. And only top creative people can produce such units.

It all seems so obvious. Inform your agency that you understand the score now. Tell your account executive that you really do not want to help his agency train neophytes. Explain to him bluntly that you are not looking for a pleasant young student who will do things *your* way, that what you damned well want is an outstanding immediate producer of exciting, dramatic, magnetic advertisements—like one of the agency's four top creative people who originally solicited your account. Leave him with this thought to chew on: that you will consider anything less than that to be professional malingering, and that it just might start you thinking about looking for a new agency connection.

"People will buy it for all sorts of reasons that they won't understand themselves, but we'll have to give them socially acceptable motives that they can verbalize. When the wife or the boss or their sons ask, 'Why did you buy that one?' our customers must have an answer. And so we've got to get going on a Here's Why You Bought It *folder to enclose with every unit we sell."*
—FROM AN AD MANAGER'S MEMO TO HIS PRESIDENT. SUBJECT: AN ELECTRIC TOOTHBRUSH.

DELUSION V

"People buy for reasons of logic"

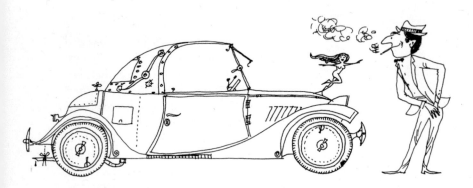

ALL THE WORLD of business seems—astonishingly—to be convinced that people buy for reasons of logic. At least, that's what they say—over and over again. "Reason-Why Copy" . . . "The Hard Sell" . . . "The Competitive Advantage" . . . "Give Them the Facts and They Will Find the Way": it's a sort of benevolent conspiracy in which the advertising profession seems to be trying to persuade the business world that it and the public to which it sells are all, all reasonable men who make their decisions on the basis of Spencer's Laws of Logic.

I happen to believe that practically nothing is bought for logical reasons. Things are almost always bought for emotional reasons and then the buyer (after he has bought) figures out some sensible reasons for having done so and persuades the boss, his wife and himself that these were his motivations. I can't prove this (so don't ask me to), but after forty years of watching sales take place I am satisfied that it is almost always so.

Even the salesman himself doesn't know why people buy from him. He fools himself for reasons of self-love, the most prevalent of all reasons. I have seen many a salesman (whose only selling asset was a wistful smile that would break the heart of a stone image) learn all the facts about his product and his competitors' until he had them at the top of his mind and on the tip of his tongue. But when he went out to sell, everybody *still* bought from him because he was "such a wonderful guy"—because of that smile. They bought because they loved him and wanted to do things for him.

But no salesman wants to believe that sort of thing; it almost makes him an object of charity. If you're a salesman, therefore, you've got to learn the facts about your product for reasons of self-respect and to give your customer excuses for doing what you have made him want to do for *your* sake. But you sell with something emotional, and all selling that I've ever seen, all advertising that was any good, was done the same way. Selling and buying are mystical things, and that is one reason why I do not believe for a minute that automation will ever replace the salesman or even really limit him.

The Eternal Triangle

The three elements that go into preparing an ad or a piece of direct mail are a case in point. By far the most important is the first of them, the copy and art, which together constitute the *Personality Element*. The second is the *Marketing Element*—the product, the price, and the offer. The third we can call the *Historical Element*: the knowledge (often of dubious authenticity) of what has worked and not worked in previous market efforts.

For a decade, say, all of a company's ads and direct mail will have the same personality. During that time the company will have been creating an Historical Element based on this single personality, consisting of certain conclusions about what works and what does not work.

Thus the Personality Element may be misleading the company. For it is perfectly possible that something that *did not* work, using the personality the company has been using, *might have worked* using another personality; or that something that *did* work, using the company's personality, *might have worked even better* using another one. Here, again, it is not the logical elements (the Historical) that are decisive, but the emotional or transitory ones (the Personality).

This theorizing about three elements in advertising applies directly to the big question of which people in a magazine audience, or on a list of good direct mail prospects, will respond to what appeals and tones. Thus certain people in the audience may be susceptible to testimonials when presented in one tone of voice, but resentful of them when presented in another. In fact,

tone of voice (or Personality) may be more important in sin-
gling out the responsive prospects from an advertising audience
than any logical factor, including the offer and the so-called history.

What Price Marketers

It is popular these days to claim that the marketing elements
are the most important in the ad, that the "offer" in direct mail
and the deal or "value" in periodical advertising are paramount—
that logic is growing more important in advertising. But recently
Madison Avenue ran an article by Jerry Fields, president of an
employment agency specializing in advertising personnel, that
would seem to contradict this. He reported that the highest salary
paid anywhere in the advertising agency business today is to the
creative director. This man makes at least 50 per cent more
than the highest salary paid to a marketing director or a market
research director, the "logic" specialists. This creative director fellow (who uses mostly emotion) makes double the highest salary
paid to the advertising director of any of his clients.

When you go into medium-sized agencies, Fields' figures show,
the creative head still makes the top money, and even in small
agencies where they don't hire creative directors, the highest
salary listed is for the copy chief, the man who makes with the
imagination.

The question asks itself. If the marketing factors were so important, why don't agencies believe in paying their top salaries to
specialists in marketing? Instead all the figures Fields has gath-
ered indicate that they pay by far their highest salaries to people
who invent and cajole: the copywriters, the creative art people,

the *Personality* creators who specialize in tone of voice, in how to say it and how it should look, rather than *what* to say and where and how often. And you can bet your bottom dollar that these people did not get where they are on the premise that *People Buy for Reasons of Logic*.

There Are No Businessmen

If people did, then the logical way, say, for a national news-weekly to appeal to its best prospects would be to address them as businessmen. I know a good deal about that from the many years I spent promoting such a magazine. In so doing, I was a member of two advertising fraternities, not just one. In promoting the magazine's advertising pages, I was pushing a product that businessmen buy for the use of their companies. In pushing the magazine's circulation, I was promoting a product that men buy for their personal use. In both cases my market consisted largely of businessmen, and after falling on my face a good many times doing what ought to come logically I concluded that *there are no businessmen*. Repeat: *THERE ARE NO BUSINESS-MEN*.

I had misjudged the nature of my market—in two ways, but not with equally important consequences. One way (the minor one) was to regard my audience as a group of men thoroughly bored with business and tired of their jobs. According to this theory, the only thing that they would read would be something provocative, amusing, entertaining. The advertising content would have to be very small indeed or they'd pitch the entire thing into the trash basket. This was a false portrait of any market of executive and professional men; and after I found that out, I labeled the thinking that led me to this mistake The Frivolous Fallacy.

My second error was more serious. This I now term The Functional Fallacy. It lies in thinking of the audience as a bunch of robots: machine-like men interested only in hard, cold, *logical* reasons for buying your product. "Buy a page in *Such and Such* and reach umpty per cent of all the executives in the coal business," or "Subscribe and get umpty-ump thousand news words a week and join the ranks of men who average umpty-ump dollars a year."

73

"Put the facts before them," claim the advertisers snared by the Functional Fallacy, *"and watch them buy."* Only they don't buy. They don't even read your advertisements or mailing pieces. They just pass them over or throw them away. Advertisers suffering from the Functional Fallacy write some of the best, most costly *unread* advertising and promotion produced in this wasteful country of ours. For the so-called businessman is neither so disgusted with facts that he won't think about them at all, nor is he so in love with them that he refuses all other nourishment. The truth is, of course, that the so-called businessman is nothing more or less than a so-called human being—usually difficult and always unpredictable.

When Is an Advertising "Boner"

But let's return to the two prime causes of this fallacious thinking. Perhaps I should define an "error" in the sense that I am using it here. I maintain that an error, mistake, or boner has been made by an advertising man or sales promotion manager when he spends good advertising or promotion money on an advertisement, direct mail unit, industrial film or other act that produces practically no reaction or only critical reaction. (If the critical reaction is almost balanced by favorable reaction, the act is probably a success; it is the ornery nature of people to kick about anything much more readily than they will applaud.)

Now, as I look back on my errors and try to divide them between the two fallacies, I find a great many more of them caused by the Functional Fallacy than by the Frivolous Fallacy. As I recall, there were actually several times as many promotion acts that flopped because they were factual, solemn, dull, and unread than because they were gadgety, wisecracking and frivolous.

And I think there are some good solid reasons behind this proportion.

In the first place, you never hear about the dull deadly flops, and so they do not cause much trouble. They merely waste the firm's money. But a single letter from an old curmudgeon of a customer saying, "I was distressed to see a firm of your standing use such theatrical devices," and you'd think the sky had fallen. And so the seven times as many dull flops never seem to be seven times as many, and the relatively few frivolous flops make a noise like a major disaster.

An Excuse for Not Thinking

There is another reason for the preponderance of functional flops. It is an astonishing fact that the forces in many companies that must approve the advertising are too often interested only incidentally in whether or not it gets read. Their real interests lie either in avoiding trouble or in immortalizing in print some company exploit or some quality of the product that they are wholly or partly responsible for—to butter their own parsnips with their directors or stockholders or their fellow members of The Young Presidents' Club.

To put it flatly, there are too many sales managers who are trying to avoid making statements in print which will push the sales force into answering a lot of new questions—even if those questions will provoke discussion that may well lead to multiplied sales. This, in my innocence, has always puzzled me. For aren't sales forces *paid* to originate and press home controversial subjects which may well smoke out business currently in competitors' hands?

And, of course, there are too many engineer-executive and production-man-executive types trying to shoe-horn into the advertising the story of technical achievements of which they are understandably proud—but which the prospect views coolly, if he will consider them at all.

Usually only the advertising professionals seem to care whether the advertising gets read, only the ad manager and his agency whether the story attracts an audience, the promotion gets across. Sometimes the president cares, and then the ad manager is really lucky. But company presidents seldom come up via advertising; they're far more likely to have a sales or production

background. Consequently, the ad manager usually has to stand
alone against the Functional Fallacy. So he has to take a calculated risk of falling into the Frivolous Fallacy—and fight dull-
ness for all he's worth, because that is the only way he can keep
the scales balanced.

This does not mean that one's non-advertising colleagues are
necessarily acting in bad faith. The sales boss, in all sincerity,
may feel that the most important thing about advertising is that
it should not cause trouble with the dealers, distributors or customers. And engineers, designers, plant managers, et cetera, may
be equally convinced that ads packed with facts and figures
must be the best kind because they are themselves so fascinated
to see their own achievements in print.

Some Blondes Are Respectable Women

It is well to keep reminding your associates of these things—
and one excellent way is to insist that *they haven't said anything
much about a man once they label him a businessman.* The use
of the stereotype "Businessman" is like the use of all stereotypes:
an excuse for *not thinking.* It is like talking about "bachelors."
All bachelors are not "neat," nor "prissy," nor "set in their ways";
nor are all bachelors seducers of women, heavy drinkers, or sophisticated men about town. And what of the talk about
"blondes"? I know blondes who are very respectable women indeed. And we all know highly successful businessmen who are
weekend painters, amateur politicians, short-wave radio hams,
bird watchers, makers of furniture and iron grillwork in their own
home workshops, and some who like to make a joyful (but not
necessarily musical) sound warbling in barber shop quartets.

What do we mean about a man when we call him a "businessman"? According to the latest census, upwards of ten million
people in America call themselves *businessmen.* They head up
so-called businessmen families, and they buy millions of dollars
worth of goods for their companies and themselves—everything
from blast furnaces to power cruisers to home air conditioners.
Some buy pigs and run great corporations; some buy pig iron and
cultivate peonies; others spend all day on their feet, like the busi-

nessman head of a huge farm enterprise; or on their buttocks at a desk. No wonder it's hard to generalize about businessmen.

What Do They Have in Common

In fact, it's hard to generalize about *anybody*. Take a typical market research situation and see what happens when you look at three businessmen *as family men* instead of executives. All three families have incomes of $12,500 a year. One is a Back Bay Boston family the other a Greenwich, Connecticut, family; the last an Astoria, Long Island, family. The family composition, age, education, in all three are exactly the same; the heads of the families are the same age and have two children each, a boy and a girl. And the wage earners of all three families are what we would call "businessmen."

The aristocratic Back Bay Boston family is virtually shabby-genteel. Its income is *below* the level it tries to keep up with. It has seen better days and will probably be spending a good deal of its money on appearances, trying to live up to the inherited traditions and responsibilities of father, grandfather, and great-grandfather. To live in the best possible taste on $12,500 a year, the family's clothes are simple, tasteful, but somewhat dowdy, and so is its limited entertaining. The head of the house plays bridge one night a week with old friends at his club—but it is not a country club. In addition to the *Atlantic* he reads books. His wife's latest big purchase was to spend $95 repairing the lace tablecloth handed down by Great-Aunt Prudence, but there is no electric washer in her home.

The smart Greenwich suburban family spends its $12,500 in still different ways. Because its income is also below the level of the group it aspires to, appearances count a lot—but they will be appearances with an eye to mobility. There will be a big bill for entertaining and for baby sitters. The husband may scrape, sandpaper and repaint the interior of their home himself but he spends freely over the weekend at the country club, and his suits are costly. In addition to a weekly newsmagazine, he reads *The New Yorker*. His wife's latest major purchase was eight modern chairs to replace those which finally collapsed after last year's dinner parties.

And, finally, the Astoria family in the workingman's community owns a good automobile on its $12,500 a year, a used car of recent vintage. Their income is just about right for the group in which they move, and so they will sometimes put off buying furniture and basic clothing (what they have are no more worn or out of date than their neighbors'.) The husband plays poker with the boys once a week and, on another night, goes bowling with his wife. He may read *Time,* but his favorite magazine is *Argosy.* Typically, Mrs. Astoria has just bought a formica-topped table for her kitchen with matching chairs (she does most of her entertaining in the kitchen).

The Only Thing in Common

About the only expense these families share in common, including their food bill, is their federal income tax. And this holds despite the fact that they would all be lumped together in a statistical summary, for few market statistics reflect the behavioral, human differences in our markets. Although the male heads of these three families are businessmen, what *do* they have in common? Will the Astoria businessman make a decision for his company on the same basis as the Back Bay businessman? Will the smart, on-the-make Greenwich executive think like (or respond to advertising like) the Back Bay man? I doubt it.

The way to advertise and promote to these men is to broadcast to them across the three wide spectrums of their human interests. Trying to reach them merely through the channel tabbed "No admittance except on business" is the hardest possible route. And there are excellent reasons why.

Let us be realistic about this matter of making a living. A job in business today is no sinecure and many a big wheel sweats like a horse when the pressure is on. It is a rare executive who breezes through his day, loving every minute of it, amiable, relaxed, open to suggestion like a happy clam on the half shell. There are moments, days, weeks, when any man in business is tense, tired, discouraged, suspicious and often downright hostile. How could it be otherwise in the savagely competitive world he occupies from nine to five?

Choosing to broadcast to him over the channel marked "Business Only" is choosing the hard way to do it, for that channel is overcrowded by your competition and by the steady static of tension. And when a man in business listens in on that channel, he does so *with his guard up*.

If you must reach a man in business at his office, try not to advertise to him as a businessman, but just as a man—an unpredictable, warmhearted, stubborn, intelligent, fickle, well-intentioned human being. Try to give him a breather from the world of facts while delivering the commercial as deftly as you can. But don't forget the commercial. For in avoiding the Functional Fallacy, you don't want to fall into the Frivolous Fallacy.

A Lot of Buddy

An example of what I mean was created in the promotion department at *Time* several years ago. It was a folder mailed to the magazine's list of advertising prospects, and it purported to be an application from a young man just out of college who wanted a job on the magazine's staff. It contained photographs mounted in a black portfolio with typewritten comments, the kind of job application you see by the hundreds. It gave a lot of facts about the magazine's audience, but it gave them in the naive words of this young applicant who insisted that a magazine reaching *this* kind of audience was the kind of magazine he wanted to work for. It evoked the kind of tenderness an older man feels when he thinks back to the mawkish mistakes he made when he first caromed into the world of business. It positioned him between what he once was and what he now knew.

The response to this mailing from men in business was overwhelming. "It really intrigued me," wrote the treasurer of a big Midwest manufacturing company, who must have had more mail than he could possibly answer, or care to. That acknowledgement is the kind a good ad man lives for. There were many others like it, all from "typical businessmen." A wine company executive confessed, "I picked up the darn thing at 5:45 yesterday afternoon when I was far too busy to read such things, only to find that I not only finished all of it but feel the urge to write you today." It was *a successful seduction*—a mailing that addressed each reader as a human being and not as one of those nonexistent, faceless, portable calculating machines called "businessmen."

Is it absurd to expect people to write and thank you for promoting them—to thank you, in effect, for selling them? Not, in my view, if you address them as human beings.

A client of mine had the courage to present his very complex story in a light and human way not long ago with very similar results. His mailing took the form of a booklet that told (with truly original and amusing illustrations) the saga of how a businessman's wife gave him the word about his own business. It was called, "Blessings on Thee, Mrs. Crabtree" and, in it, Mr. Crabtree comes home late for a fine dinner of *Pompano Veronique* with a pleasant little *Pouilly Fumé* that his wife has assembled for him. Understandably miffed, the little lady tells him a few fundamental truths about himself while he stuffs on slightly overdone fish and cream sauce. In the process of telling him what an old-fashioned bore he is turning into, she sells him on the advertiser's product, one that he has been reluctant to buy for his business. At one point she mentions that there are four million dollars worth of something or other in the country—and, expressing his wonder with his mouth full, Mr. Crabtree mutters, "Four billion dollars is a lod of buddy." " 'Million,' dear—not 'billion,' " she corrects him: You get the idea.

At any rate, four thousand prospects wrote to the sender of that mailing piece to say how much they liked it. Inevitably, it increased sales; even the sales department admitted *that*.

You Have to Keep Shifting Around

Of course, all mailings cannot be successful; some lay a most infertile egg. There will always be some people in the audience who won't like what the ad man does, but he has to figure that they *ought* to like the *next* thing he does. He has to keep shifting around in the *way* he tells his story—on the principle that there are many different kinds of men on his mailing list and he should try to please all of them some of the time rather than some of them all of the time.

If his ads or direct mail keep plugging away always in the same tone of voice, he is in effect talking over and over to the same kind of man—the man on his list who happens to *like* that tone of voice. He is reaching some of his prospects all the time and neglecting the rest—perhaps six, seven, eight out of every ten. He can avoid that formula for failure by directing one advertisement or direct mail piece to the facetious-minded, the next one to the serious-minded, the next to the man who likes to know what others use, the next to the rugged individualist, etc. And if he addresses them as human beings, not businessmen, doctors, engineers or teachers, he has a good chance of getting them to listen to his story.

Shallow or Deep? That Is the Question

Looking at each unit of promotion as if it were a magazine in miniature, it is obvious that every ad or direct mail piece, like every magazine, should have both an editorial and an advertising content. The editorial content is the *allure* which moves the recipient to want to read the unit of promotion whether he is a prospect or not. It is the nostalgia in the job applicant mailing or the wit in an amusing piece of copy or art. It is that element in the promotion that appeals to the human being rather than to the businessman. The advertising content, of course, is the self-adulation the advertiser wants to get across, or the news about the prices, facts and figures on his Giant-Crushing-Grinder machines.

Almost no promotion, however, is all editorial or all advertising, and here a principle emerges. If your problem requires making only a simple and shallow advertising impression, you can afford to make your promotion mostly editorial in content and thus tempt a large proportion of your market to read it. But if you require a deep advertising impression, you can afford only a small editorial content, and you must be resigned to reaching only a fraction of your potential readers.

The Container Corporation's advertising remains one of the best examples of getting everybody to notice your advertising by making it 99 per cent editorial. These attractive ads, familiar to people everywhere, have done a first-rate job of establishing the name of their sponsor. Had they tried to do more, the Container Corporation would probably have had to be satisfied with a much smaller readership.

So would the Telephone Company, which has much the same problem. It doesn't have to tell people what a telephone is; it just wants to keep them thinking about it. So, for years, its major advertising featured engaging drawings of children which appeal to practically everybody, or photos of the wrinkled delight on grandma's face when you call her long distance. What little had to be said about using the telephone didn't have to be read; you got the point without it. A light advertising impression was being made on a great many people.

A deep advertising impression, on the other hand, may mean parading your ad before hundreds of thousands of people in the hope that the few hundred who are actively and immediately in the market for your product will read it thoroughly. Hearing aids are a good example. They are advertised in many media and all of the ads feature the word "Deaf" in one form or another. The word selects out of the general readership those people whose immediate need dovetails with the product. Once the deafened person (or a relative) is attracted to the copy, the small type takes over, piling detail on detail and claim on counterclaim.

Shallow or deep, it's all the same to the advertising man. Different needs merely require different tools. But, over all needs, like a writing in the sky, loom the words of an old Roman named Lactantius. Lactantius said a few centuries ago, "Anything pleasant easily persuades, and while it gives pleasure, it fixes itself in the heart."

It Tickles, Needles and Nudges

There just isn't anything pleasant in listening to talk or reading copy addressed to you "as a businessman." In fact, *there are no businessmen*—only individuals with different thumbprints and different hobbies and different habits of making buying decisions. All the logic in Christendom won't persuade them to listen, read or buy without that little touch of seduction we have talked about before.

And television is coming to know this. More, perhaps than any other medium these days, it tickles and needles and nudges its audiences into doing the things which it began by arguing with them about or by absurdly demonstrating. Ironically enough, the dog foods seem to be airing the most civilized commercials right now—some are actually little masterworks of humor. Levy's Jewish Rye Bread, with its rubber-faced sandwich eaters of every ethnic background, is high on the list of humorous, appealing commercials here in the East. And on the West Coast even

the church is using humor to promote Sunday attendance. Although most of the cigarettes limp along either with vacuous inanities or forced fellowship (where they mingle with the beers), the detergents are employing a sort of fantastic silliness that seems calculated to seduce exactly the kind of women they are after.

Only the proprietary medicines and the deodorants (Rollaids, Bufferin, Ice Blue Secret, etc.) seem to be sticking to cold, reason-why logic with diagrams of throats, stomachs, and armpits and statements like, "absorbs up to 47 per cent of its own weight in acids." Fantasy, whimsy and humor (all handmaidens of seduction) rank higher and higher on the air waves from the Hertz driver dropping out of the sky to the man of the house fruitlessly racing through the streets trying to get a boxed pizza home before it cools to make Chef Boy-Ar-Dee's point that their way is an easier way. I wonder when or if print advertising will ever catch up and stop dead-panning its way through our new devil-may-care world.

Buying Is a Very Unserious Matter

In fact, products that do not take themselves too seriously in their advertising are the realistic ones these days. For as our affluent society becomes more so and its choice of brands, models, colors and prices multiplies, it gets increasingly apparent that the act of buying most things is *a very unserious matter*. It all reminds me of the expression on the face of Henry R. Luce on one occasion when, after he had made some high-flown, lengthy statement about the future of *Time*, one of his more irreverent colleagues said to him, "Oh, come off it, Harry; it's only a magazine. And most people don't give much of a damn about even their *favorite* magazine." After he had caught his breath, the great man said, "What do they care *more* about?" (He was always curious, always the journalist.)

"Oh," laughed his tormentor, "their favorite woman, their favorite drink, their favorite food, their favorite chair—and even," he added winsomely, "their favorite boss." And, as he was demonstrating, people don't even take *those* too seriously any more.

"Winston Tastes Good Like a Cigarette Should"
. . . "Makes Your Washer Work Like It's Ten
Feet Tall" . . . "While You're Up, Get Me a
Grant's" . . . "Better Products for Better Living
Through Chemistry"

DELUSION VI

"Advertising is information"

A POLOGISTS FOR ADVERTISING are fond of justifying its existence on the grounds that nothing so effectively transfers information between maker and user. That advertising (most advertising) conveys *some* information is undeniable. That such is its primary purpose, however, is absurd.

The following situation is taken from life in an advertising agency. (But it isn't taken very *far* from life; the product and some of the lines are changed—that is all.)

The problem was to find a headline for an advertisement describing a new automatic washer. The client said that the main thing to stress was the fact that it was "the most ingenious invention the field had ever known." The account executive thought that this was a great statement and that the ad should feature a picture of the client making it. The copy director said that nobody cared how ingenious the machine was; women were interested only in what it did for *them*. (He had an idea that involved showing a picture of the week's wash of a single, active, ten-year-old boy with the headline, *"A Peck of Wash for Peck's Bad Boy."*) The art director was enamored of a layout showing an abstract design based on a moth-wing valve in the machine: "An Aztec-like motif in white on gray-blue," as he described it. . . .

Unexpectedly, the creative director wanted to do a research ad (to show the agency president that, despite rumors, he could *so* get along with the new research director). . . . The research department wanted to base the ad on the result of motivational depth interviews with 112 women, the consensus of which (interpreted by the new director) was, "A woman takes her wash out of a washer and examines it in the same spirit that she looks first upon the face and form of her newborn babe." . . . But the traffic man on the account pointed out that the same Freudian interpretation had been used by a flour manufacturer to describe the way in which a woman takes a cake out of the oven. . . . And so they took most of the Starch out of the wash and compromised on a headline to please the client, *"The Most Ingenious Washing Idea Since Soap."*

Object: *To Communicate Pride*

That's a pretty good, "attention-arousing" headline—but is it information? It wasn't written to communicate anything except the pride of the maker in his product. The part of the headline that is effective "*—Since Soap*" has a half-smile in it; it charms and titillates rather than informs. The copy chief, with his Peck's Bad Boy line, and the art director, with his Aztec motif were trying to be clever or charming or both. They were, in short, trying to *seduce*—which is the true purpose of all advertising.

It is, in fact, a lot easier to seduce a person than to transfer information to him. For people resist being instructed while they do not resist being amused and charmed and teased. What is more, true instruction takes time and money. To educate a prospect (or, harder still, to re-educate him) is a long-term effort,

often too expensive to be worth it. In consequence, both the advertiser and the advertisee con themselves into taking the easier route—they enter into a seductive relationship and call it a relationship of logic. The advertiser doesn't want to admit that he is weaving a spell and the advertisee doesn't want to admit that he is buying under that spell. Face is saved outrageously on both sides by calling the little *affaire du charme* a matter of factual communication. And so that is the way it is discussed and everyone is happy.

The Pejorative Adjectives

Webster describes the verb "seduce" as the process of "leading or drawing astray as into an evil, foolish or disastrous course, tempting or enticing." Let us beg, for the moment, the question of motive, the matter of whether the advertiser intends to lead the reader of his ad into an "evil, foolish or disastrous course." Whatever his intentions, the use of all three of these pejorative adjectives might be justified in describing an advertiser who tempts a man to buy a new TV set when he hasn't enough money to keep his kids in school or feed and clothe them properly.

Let's do no more than mention cigarette and liquor advertising here—but rather, while in the shadow of those adjectives, let's consider what might be adjudged one of the most *un*seductive kinds of advertising. Its target is the small manufacturer whom it tempts or entices into buying a new and costly piece of heavy equipment that he doesn't really need and which puts him in hock to the manufacturer for so large a sum that he eventually goes out of business. The ad or mailing piece itself may not have a misstatement in it. As far as it goes, it may tell the simple truth (but only those truths that are to the advantage of the advertiser). It will not mention, for example, that maintenance costs on this unit are higher than on competitive models (why should it?), nor that a newer model will be shortly introduced that operates on half the power or that only a large output-demand really justifies the cost of a piece of equipment like this. Nevertheless, because of what it doesn't say and because of the implications of these omissions (that the points they would have made are not important), the advertisement becomes a seduction, complete with those three unpleasant adjectives.

Consider the Foul-Mouthed Buyer

But let us ponder also the great number of ads that tempt a buyer to do something that actually does him some good. For the point of these examples is not whether the enticement, temptation or seduction leads to good or evil, but that it *is* an enticement, temptation or seduction and not primarily what it pretends to be —a piece of information of use to the reader. Even the ad that keeps a foul-mouthed buyer rinsing with a mouthwash that temporarily relieves his halitosis, even the Advertising Council ads that make people aware of the dangers of venereal disease or get them contributing to the Heart Fund, even the Dairy Association ads that shoe-horn in a little milk between the Cokes that so many malnourished rich kids live on—all these get whatever desirable results they get by seduction, by teasing, cajoling, intriguing the reader into doing what he ought to do.

Even the most ethical advertiser couldn't care less what happens to the buyer of his product after it is purchased—as long as the product lives up to what he actually claims for it in writing (not by implication) and as long as it doesn't get him into trouble with the authorities. There are those who will say that this doesn't hold for many articles that live on repeat business rather than on the initial purchase—articles like razor blades, detergents, gasolines. But, even here, the object is to get the original sale, to seduce the prospect into trying the product. For in these fields all the competing makers tell their half-truths at about the same rate; they all make about equally effective (or ineffective) products so that nobody can do very much about it if the product doesn't live up to the claim.

You'll Switch and Be No Better Off

And so when the stainless steel blade does *not* give a practically limitless number of perfect shaves and the detergent does *not* take the grime out of the neckband of the shirt and the gas

does not make the old jalopy spring forward like a feral beast of the jungle, you can always switch brands and *do no better.* As for the bad will that is supposed to follow the purchase of a product that does not live up to its promises (and is therefore supposed to cut into the repeat business), it is like your dissatisfaction with the U.S. mails. If you don't like the company, give your business to someone else.

Every now and then, of course, some firm really gets the drop on its competitors and, for a while, information has its day. For a short period there was only one brand of stainless steel razor blades and it was important to know which one it was. For a time (only a short one) Oldsmobile had automatic shifting all to itself. But very soon everyone gets aboard and we are back where we were, all seducing with the same body, exaggerating at the same rate and the devil take the hindmost; in this case, the customer.

Too Many Brands in the Pod

Perhaps the cause is that our affluent society supports too many choices to make simply informational advertising effective. We have so much money to spend that six or twenty brands can prosper in markets where there are only two or three basic differences possible in the product being offered. And they all get by for reasons they don't dare feature in their advertising—because the package design of one is more appealing to the snob trade, because the color of another tickles the risibilities of those with homosexual tendencies, because there is a rumor that the maker of a third product won't hire Negroes (big sale in the South) or that he won't buy his oil from the Arabs (big sale among the

Jews) or that he puts more "dope" into his soft drink than the others (big sale among dopes). At any rate, caught without real differentiations to advertise (or blessed with differences they don't dare advertise), a great many advertisers just keep drawing their products longer and sleeker until they outrage every law of perspective or keep faking their TV commercials so obviously that even a feebleminded schoolboy could see through them or persist in describing their oversize art books or perfumes or resorts in phrases that sound like the ravings of those who eat hallu-cinogenic mushrooms.

Recently the comic strip called "Penny," widely distributed by Publishers' Newspaper Syndicate, featured the following dia-logue with appropriate cartoons:

Penny: What are you reading, father?
Father: Scientific fiction.
Penny: Space shot to the end of the universe?
Father: Nothing so simple. How to grow vegetables like the pictures in seed catalogues.

Are these vendors under the impression that they are giving their prospects more information in the form of their hyperbole? As my current favorite juvenile would say, "Gadzooks! Of course not."

Pain, Pain, Pain

The object is to seduce. Listen to the music of the Anacin com-mercial as the pendulum swings, swings, swings and the voice talks about pain, pain, pain and relief, relief, relief. Hypnotism. Absorb the words "careful, punctual, clean" as they are repeated over and over in the KLM ads prepared by David Ogilvy—the careful Dutch, the clean Dutch, the punctual Dutch. Any real evidence that these planes are cleaner, more punctual, more care-fully serviced than the British, American, French or Israeli planes? Gadzooks! Of course not. "I'm particular. How about you?" asks Pall Mall; "I'd rather fight than switch," says Tarey-ton; and a voice adds, "No Scotch improves the flavor of water like Teacher's." Any information here? Any proof that Pall Mall smokers are really more particular than Herbert Tareyton smok-ers who, in turn, are more loyal than drinkers of Teacher's Scotch? And *who says* that Teacher's improves the flavor of water in some unique way? Even if so, is this a good thing? How is a flavor "improved" for everyone? Some like it sweet; some like it dry and some like it with ginger ale.

There are no answers to these questions, because logic and data and information have nothing whatever to do with the case. If nobody says that they'd rather fight than switch from Tareytons except the advertising department—and people *like* the line (it doesn't matter why)—then the line's a successful seduction. It was new and it caught on; and therein lies a sale.

The Essence of Seduction

The truth is that the essence of seduction is the unexpected, the unusual—and that advertising now and always suffers from *too little originality*. Do you know what it is that makes that new girl seductive? It's the new curve of her lips, the new way she has of batting her eyes at you in admiration, the new way she whispers your name. What seduces you into taking this job instead of that, assuming they both have the same responsibilities and pay the same? A new personality in the boss, a new location in a more interesting area, a new wrinkle in your duties, a new chance to take a winter instead of a summer vacation. The fresh, the new, the original—that is the essence of seduction.

What do I mean by the original in advertising? I mean *originality of Format:* printing your message on a piece of silk; or making it look like a cocktail napkin; or mailing it in a little, plush-lined jeweler's case; or inventing the gatefold page for an advertisement in *Life*.

I mean *originality of Timing*: timing an announcement that you are opening a new office in Cairo to arrive in the mail the day that Nasser comes to Washington to talk to the President—timing an ad about a sale of trousseau underwear or bridesmaid's frippery to appear the day Grace Kelly marries Prince Rainier in Monaco—timing a price cut to tread on the heels of a presidential appeal to hold the line on inflation.

I mean, always, *originality of Copy*: a pair of poultry shears offered in a department store newspaper ad. Says the turkey: "Please give me something to dismember me by!" Or a book of gossip described as containing lines that "tickle and needle and nudge." Or Lanson Champagne's use of just one line in its ads, "There's only one question—can you afford it?"

I mean, always, *originality of Art:* a mailing to secretaries on St. Valentine's Day in which the main illustration is a five-cent stamp surrounded by a frieze of cupids, hearts and flowers—an illustration in a Christmas ad for Sony television sets, showing a very fat man lying in bed on his back, watching the screen of a tiny TV set sitting on his stomach—a look of idiotic contentment on his face.

I mean *originality of Attitude:* the unexpected tone of voice, the unpredictable (and therefore arresting) phrase, drawing or name. Qantas Air Lines naming its big, beautiful jet-engine planes "Sam" and presenting a kangaroo as a prize to the winner of their name-selecting contest . . . Container Corporation's inspired technique of selling cartons by publishing striking abstract paintings and pearls of wisdom from the writings of the greatest philosophers and thinkers . . . The Manufacturers Hanover Trust, a staid, dignified organization in a traditionally stuffy field, advertising itself on television with animated cartoons that look as if they were done by a not particularly gifted child.

The Beard, The Leopard and the Eye-Patch

I mean *originality of Audience:* the department store mailing its sale announcements to the employees of its suppliers; *The New Yorker* mailing subscription letters to all the old ladies in Dubuque. (The first line of that letter should read, of course, "Honest, ladies, we were only kidding.")

I mean *originality of Medium:* a liniment, famous as a stiff-neck remedy, using skywriting . . . lighters advertising on match books that say "Aren't matches a nuisance?" . . . Douglas Leigh, producer of mammoth spectaculars, spreading word of his service by mailing a message engraved on the head of a pin.

I mean *originality of Association:* Commander Whitehead's beard and Schweppes . . . the leopard and vodka . . . the eye-patch and the Hathaway shirt . . . the shuffle and Teaberry gum.

There's never enough of this kind of thing in advertising. Some of its best professional writers, like their opposite numbers in Hollywood, are prone to stay too long with an idea that has worked. If one Civil War movie makes a lot of money, there follows a clutch of Civil War movies, and the last of them are invariably awful duds. It's the same in advertising. Somebody dreams up a new format or copy approach and the imitators imitate it to death (Examples: magazines using sheets of phony stamps in their circulation mail; everybody comparing his product to a tiger.)

I used to have a sign on the bulletin board of my office that read: "Let's never the hell do it *that* way again." And I meant it.

But it isn't easy. Business managers invariably put their weight (and it tends to be considerable) behind the so-called tried-and-true appeals. Only they won't be true forever—or even for very long—because the essence of seduction is to be original. But what *will* get and hold the attention of the new prospects? Certainly not information; they couldn't care less. Nor self-praise, the unpleasant bane of so much advertising. Only a brighter, more civilized, more adult, ever more original form of seduction will do it.

Charles L. Whittier, retired vice president and chairman of the plans board of Young & Rubicam, has said it very well: "The beginning of greatness is to be different. Conversely, the beginning of mediocrity is to be the same. Similarity flourishes like weeds. But differences must be cultivated like rare and fragile flowers. The successful production of great advertising is a never-ending resistance to similarity; a constant struggle to avoid the usual; a continuous effort to provide new ideas, to illustrate them with freshness and to express them with originality."

Sing a song of probity:
A pocketful of wry.
Four and twenty blackguards
Baked in a pie.
When the pie was opened,
The finks began to sing.
Wasn't that a dainty dish . . . ?

DELUSION VII

"You can be in the advertising business and keep your integrity"

A RECENT ISSUE of the New York *Times* carried the following interesting testimony on the advertising world:

A former executive of an advertising agency testified reluctantly in court yesterday that a highly successful promotion campaign for a reducing pill had been dishonest.

The witness, Richard King, television producer for the Regimen Tablet account at Kastor, Hilton, Chesley, Clifford & Atherton, admitted in Brooklyn Federal Court that he knew models used in commercials were on severe diets. Yet the scripts he provided for them attributed the weight loss to the pills alone 'without dieting' . . .

It has been said that "an advertising man is born in a fog and dies on the first clear day." There is a lot in that aphorism, but, if it's so foggy on Madison Avenue, how did it get that way? I have a theory.

Back in the days when most advertising was spoken and most people didn't know how to read, the public crier announced the availability of many goods and services. He survives today in the radio-television announcer—but with an important difference. Whereas the public crier merely offered goods and services; the radio-TV announcer cozens, wheedles, persuades, charms. He *sells.*

I suppose, in the best of all possible worlds, goods and services might still be merely offered. But came the industrial revolution and, with it the Manchester mills, the steam printing press and the world's first cheap source of newsprint for the mass distribution of words. Things have never been the same since.

Power was what industry was waiting for, and when its new machinery began to bring more and more cheap consumer goods into the market, industry gradually found that it needed advertisement producers to sell the products of the machines almost as much as it needed mechanics to keep the machines running.

In the long slide of time from the public crier to the radio-TV announcer, a new kind of man has developed—part journalist, part peddler, part lawyer: the *Special Pleader*.

In the movie, *Lawrence of Arabia*, somebody says to the hero (a great Special Pleader if I ever heard one), "Because you have always told half-truths, you have forgotten where the truth is." Every member of the Advertising Establishment spends most of his working hours concocting half-truths and then trying to distribute them as widely and persuasively as possible. This is his job. He is not paid to tell the whole truth or even to know it. Usually he isn't told it. When he comes across facts that weaken or fail to strengthen his case, he automatically ignores them, buries or eliminates them, not only from his thinking but from his consciousness as well. By working hard at this assignment (and it isn't an easy one), he gradually succeeds at it. And so he forgets where the truth is, masters his half-truths, and his income begins to climb.

The Special Pleader

Now, let it be clearly understood that I see nothing wrong about this from the point of view of advertising. Nor are these remarks intended to be a plea for integrity in advertising, if, by integrity, we mean telling the whole truth. For advertising,. by definition, is a special pleader. Nobody in his right mind really believes an advertisement or a promotion piece; not really, not the way you believe your father or a good friend. Nobody with

any sense expects to find the whole truth in an advertisement any more than he expects a man applying for a job to describe his shortcomings and more serious faults. Who is willing to denigrate his own product or service except a fool? There's bound to be something wrong (or imperfect) with almost anything. In short, *the half-truth is the essence of advertising*.

But what impact has this fact upon the advertising man? The need to deal only with the truths that further his purpose cannot help carrying over into his life outside his work. As he proceeds along the path of his career, he is likely to become less and less real, more and more lopsided ("half-assed" is a good phrase for it.) When the school teacher goes home, she tends to treat the members of her family as if they were children. The man who is paid to listen to complaints all day long for the Bon Ton Department Store continues to be a receiving apparatus for his friends' grievances after hours. The professional advertising man tends to examine his company, superiors, colleagues, friends, community, nation, civilization, in the same way. He seeks only the things he wants to find, only what he can use in his continuing campaign to make himself a contented, effective company and family man. The following dialogue at Dawson's Steak Pub may illustrate what I mean:

She: How's the new job?

He: Great. Just great.

She: All shaken down? Snug as a bug?

He: Not quite. But really, Dorine—I mean it—they're a swell bunch.

She: Sure. How do you like your boss?

He: Very much. Very much indeed. He's a sweet, sweet guy. Asked me out to his place for dinner Tuesday. Met his wife and kid, and we talked until midnight about trout flies. We're going to be real friends.

She: Like you and George?

He: Now, Dorine; this is different.

She: Remember how George wouldn't wiggle a finger to help you get a new job after they fired you? Not a phone call, even.

He: It wasn't their fault. They lost a lot of business.

She: They must have got it back fast judging by the billing figures. You were there seven years, Joe, and you were prexie's special pet. They didn't have to lay you off. (*Silence.*)

He: Well, I'm still pushing forty and I've got a new job for more money. So what's lost?

She: Nothing much, I guess. Except—

He: Except what? Except what, Dorine?

She: Well, except that I hate to hear you pulling that "swell bunch-sweet guy" routine again. You're setting yourself up to get hurt just like before, buddy boy.

He: You're hard—a hard, hard woman.

She: Yes. And you're soft—a soft, soft man. (*Silence.*)

He: Well, how do you expect me to feel about a new job? You think I should *hate* everybody?

(*Silence.*)

He: Like Bill Squire? He's contact on Snaps. Should I tell Bill to peddle his papers when he asks me to lunch and spends the whole time telling me how I'm the first creative guy they ever put on this account that he can talk to? Should I kick his teeth in because he pays for the lunch and memos the boss that my layouts are just what Snaps needed? Is that being a nice guy or isn't it? He didn't *have* to do that, did he?

She: Nope. But he might just have an angle. You ought to know by now that the kind of love-each-other stuff you've been talking is a lot of goop. A job is a job. You do your work; you keep your antennae wriggling and your nose clean, and if you have to love somebody, try your wife or a girl friend. Not me. I'm too hard.

He: I can't work like that. I have to like the people I work with. I have to know them and understand them and let them understand me as warm human beings.

She: But why? You know it's phony. You just told me the other day that nobody from Cheapside, Fewlett has even called you for a drink since you left the dump. Out of sight; out of mind. But last year at this time your evenings and weekends were full of Cheapsiders. It's going to be no different at Barret & Karp, Joe. The people you work with aren't your friends, except by accident. They don't really give a damn about anything but getting ahead or holding on. And the higher up they are the more frightened they are. They certainly don't give a damn about *you*.

He: (*Standing up*) I'm not going to listen to this. It's—*subversive*. You'll unfit me for my job.

She: Oh, tush.

(*He walks off.*)

She: And here's Dorine, stuck with the check again. Waiter! Waiter —another martini, please! And put a bitter aloe in it.

Such is the human condition along Wilshire Boulevard and Madison and North Michigan Avenues and in any or all haunts of the U. S. Advertising Establishment, for that matter. In this context the advertising man tends more and more to see the boss as a Genius or a Sweet Guy or a Dedicated Corporate Servant, a Privilege to Work For (the old so-and-so!). His siblings are all Nice Fellows, he insists, as he ducks and squirms to evade the daggers aimed at his back. The little woman (that nagger!) is a Great Gal; his suburb is the Finest Little Community that ever skimped on a school appropriation or segregated a minority group. And he believes all this, just as he believes, if he represents a national business magazine (like *Newsweek* or *Time* or *U. S. News*), that none but highly-incomed executives read his magazine; that it has the highest editorial standards in the field, and that there is absolutely no difference in the attention given an ad on page three of the book and the ad on page 64. Position? What has position to do with it?

What Price Self-Deception?

And what, you may ask, is the harm in all this deception? Each man, to earn a living, must give a part of himself, must trade something to society for his board and keep. The ditch digger contributes his physical strength; the doctor, his medical knowledge; the pastor, his spiritual energy. And so the advertising man must give—what? His technical knowledge of marketing patterns? . . . of research? . . . of copy and art? Yes, but unlike the laborer, the doctor, or the pastor, the conditions of his profession require the value put upon his special knowledge to be second to something else. What he is *really* paid for is a quality that we might term "Eclectic Amnesia," the ability to select (like a radar beam scanning a field) the weaknesses in his product and then to bury them in his forgettery, so that he can concentrate on what's left for his advertising and promotion campaigns. The better he does this, the more he prospers; if he cannot do it, he is fired. He alone of those I have mentioned, must, in a sense, blind himself to earn his livelihood.

The ditch digger, doctor and divine can also blind themselves to certain truths in their professions and, in many cases, advance their incomes and prestige by skimping or passing over certain truths distasteful to others—including their superiors. But they have a choice; they do not necessarily *have* to. They can just do run-of-the-mill jobs of digging, healing and comforting, and get by. But the advertising-promotion man *must* deceive his market just to hold his job. He can never tell the whole truth; it is better if he cannot even see it.

Anyone is entitled to say at this juncture, "There are others who must deal in half-truths to make their living. What about the salesman, the politician?" Henry Wotton once described an ambassador as, "An honest man sent to lie abroad for the good of his country." Yes, the salesman and politician are in much the same class as is the advertising-promotion man—and, for that matter, the ambassador who, in truth, is also a politician. But notice that the ambassador is called an *honest* man who is sent abroad to *lie*. He may be nothing of the sort, but that's the way the world looks at his job. Nobody ever called the advertising-promotion man or the politician "honest" men, and this difference may well be because the true liar must never forget where the truth is. He doesn't dare to, for he must constantly avoid it. But those of us who have to deal with the half-truth can never be honest in the ambassadorial sense. To convince our audiences, we must seduce them—and to make a good job of *that,* we must first seduce ourselves.

Advice to an Ad Director

This necessity to choose part of a truth and then treat it as if it were a whole truth is in the very essence of an advertising job. It runs through everything—from the creation of ads to the relationships among ad men. Consider for a moment the contradictory views that can bedevil a company advertising director who is trying his best to work with the agency serving his company. Here are five pairs of *directly opposed recommendations*, all of which are continuously being urged upon him as the *only* way in which to handle himself. Some of these alternates are strongly indicated by his own management—others have the revolutionary rasp of the old pro in the job advising the neophyte. In reviewing them, it might be well to keep in mind an utterance of that great man, Henry Haskins: "Both sides of a question do not belong to the poor question at all, but to the opposing views that bedevil it."

1A. Give the agency all the credit

It is excellent strategy to credit your agency with all the good ideas and all the execution that turns out well. This endears you to your agency—and you wouldn't want to antagonize a group of men that has sold your boss a bill of goods, would you? Besides, if you keep insisting that you and your people don't do anything except "liaison" between the agency and your management, pretty soon your boss will stop believing you.

"It isn't possible he doesn't do *anything*," he'll say to himself one day. "He must do *something*." And from there it's only a step to his saying, "I'll bet he does *so* do everything—and he's giving the agency all the credit just to save me the trouble of looking for another agency. What a man! I must double his bonus."

1B. Don't give the agency any credit at all

Be a perfectionist. Raise hell, hell, hell. Keep sending copy back; ask for ever-new media schedules; turn down all agency research as "superficial," "inadequately based," "destructively conceived." Send your boss evidence demonstrating agency inadequacies: bad copy, overcharges, details on traffic snafus. Your goal should be a new agency every year.

Lose no opportunity to show how indispensable you are. Isn't it true that "Nobody from *outside* can speak for our company" —that "to understand our problems you've got to live with them twenty-four hours a day"? What's more, there is a company way of saying things, a certain tone (a *timbre*, if you will), and only somebody who's been around a while and has your sensitivity, talents, and gift for communicating can express that tone. Make this clear to your boss and to the agency. Everything must bear the stamp of your style or it just won't sound like good old Bell Corp.

* * *

2A. Cultivate your agency's top officials

Ask them to dinner. Have cocktails with the agency prexy and even the board chairman, if he'll let you. *You* pay the bills— or at least pay half the time. Insist on it. "This was *my* idea, J.C. I learn an awful lot every time I see you. It's worth it, dammit."

Are you socially connected? Most top agency people are social climbers. That agency senior vice president, for instance—the one who practically lives with your top management. Get your Aunt Agatha to invite him and his wife to dinner; he'll be grateful. And he'll mention it back at the shop. Remember, your agency's upper echelon is one of the best pipelines you've got to the top officials of your own company. Make them *love* you.

2B. Cultivate only your agency product group

To get the best out of your agency, align yourself with the people who do the work on your account: the marketers, planners, writers, artists. Create a workers' front in contrast to the fair-haired boys who do the contact on your level and above.

Work with your jacket off and your tie loosened; see that you're over at the agency a lot, in the art department, down on your knees looking at layouts. Be seen often at the bar and pizza joint patronized by the agency's working stiffs. Have your traffic man out to the house for beer and *bocci* Sunday afternoon, but turn down all invitations from your account man.

* * *

3A. Keep your management posted all the way

Every time you talk with anyone in your agency, send a memo to your boss at once, reporting what was said, done or decided. Better than that, memo your boss *before* you talk to the agency; memo him the day after about how it went; and memo him again at the first reaction from the agency.

Remember that no two people ever see an accident the same way—and you'd better tell your story first. Did I hear someone say that two men of goodwill meeting with the same objective is not an accident? You haven't been paying attention, mister.

3B. Let the agency keep your management posted

The Conference Report is the ultimate weapon in the agency's arsenal as it wages its never-ending war to prove to its clients that "Without Us, Nothing." There's no point in fighting it. It works like this:

Assume that the subject of your meeting is a newspaper ad. You have written the copy and decided that it should run in the New York *Times,* the Chicago *Tribune* and the St. Louis *Post-Dispatch.* The Conference Report from the agency to your superiors will describe the meeting as follows:

"We met with the advertising director to discuss a newspaper ad. The agency submitted a list of twelve papers in four cities from which a schedule of three papers in three cities was finalized. A piece of copy was discussed and approved. The ads will appear August 14."

Notice the passive grammatical construction in which your contribution to this affair has been buried. The impression is that everything was done by the agency. This stylistic device is known to grammarians as "the agency passive pre-emptive." It's a beaut!

Relax in the presence of the agency Conference Report. Step aside and let nature take its course. This amounts to surrendering unconditionally—often a very wise move, especially if you'd rather work for your agency than for your present employer.

* * *

4A. Be patient with an inept product group

You can build an esprit de corps, more precious than rubies among the people working on your account at the agency—if you will but control your natural impatience and testiness. Be grateful when not too experienced writers, layout men, traffic men, merchandisers are assigned to you. They are raw material to be trained and fitted to the needs of your account like the branches of an espaliered pear tree—and you're the gardener that can do it, especially with your green thumb. An agency group developed patiently by a wise and understanding ad director can burnish his reputation and create relationships that will bring increasing dividends with the years.

4B. Don't let the agency stick you with a bunch of tyros. Insist on the pros.

When it comes to getting the right agency team together, the client that squeaks the loudest is the first to get the grease. Any agency, if you sit still for it, will attach its dogs to your leash: the halt and the lame, the about-to-be fired; the wide-eyed, somewhat talented, smashingly inexperienced beginners. Don't stand for it. Kick and scream. Threaten to go over the head of your account supervisor to the agency prexy. You've got better things to do than to wipe the chins of a bunch of beginners who will be taken off your account the minute you teach them something. You're entitled to people who can start producing the minute they get on your account. You're not a pedagogue; you're an expediter— and if your agency is going to assign a bunch of know-nothings to your account, you'll start looking for a new agency.

* * *

5A. Always work through your agency contact man

An advertising agency is a sensitive, organic entity that is kept focused on any practical problem only with the greatest diffi- culty. It squirms like a river of eels between two sandbanks—one called Creativity and one Organization. Both banks must be con- tinuously shored up or the whole slippery marinade oozes out of the channel and becomes a marsh.

Your contact man has been put at his place in the organization chart to keep the river in its course and make it useful to you. To scramble the metaphor unbearably, his purpose is to funnel your needs and instructions to the product group at the agency after sharpening them on the whetstone of his creativity and re- shaping them on the anvil of his advertising expertise. He is the one man at the agency best qualified to find the right person there to do any piece of work or thinking for you. Consequently, you should transmit all business through him and make sure he sits in on every talk you have with the agency's working people.

5B. Don't let the agency contact department isolate you from your group

The idea that an idea can be carried like a box of Kleenex from one brain to another by a third brain and arrive unsoiled, unrumpled and undiminished is meretricious. And many a prom- ising client-agency relationship has been smeared into meaning- lessness by the agency's insistence that this idiotic procedure be honored.

Insist on face-to-face sessions with the agency specialists as- signed to your problems; get in there with them and make sure they know what's in your mind. If your account man can sit in, fine; if he can't, let him get an assistant or something so that he isn't off baby-sitting his other accounts when he ought to be with you.

Probably you will get into trouble with the agency by cutting across their lines; so set up your defenses by sending your boss a memo-in-detail before you take this tack. Tell him what you're up to and why, so that he's all set when the agency asks him to lunch, with you in mind for the main course.

No Room for Neutrals

It is obvious that these paired philosophies will be only blunted thorns in the side of the ad director who has full authority over his agency. His name, however, is anything but legion. In all other cases, the ad director and the agency are rivals competing for the same prize, the confidence of the boss advertiser. In such a spot a man can choose either to engage his agency in ferocious combat or

surrender to it, but he cannot elect to play a neutral role. For he who flies the banner of tattletale gray on this battlefield loses either his self-respect or his job.

Or half his self-respect and half his job. For sad to say, we find many ad directors forever asking themselves, "Is it better to live on my knees or die on my feet?"—postponing their answers for years, existing ignobly in a sort of shambling crouch. It is a spectacle from which we must avert our eyes; it makes radiant neither the image of advertising nor of mankind. For there is only one real answer to the ancient knees or feet dilemma: you have to stand up—to the agency. And if you lose, if you cannot win and hold your boss's confidence, quit. Go find another boss.

Bury the Opposition

The point of these recent pages should, by now, be sharp as a serpent's tooth: No two of the paired statements can possibly be true at the same time. And yet there are as many supporters in advertising for the A arguments as for the B's. In fact, the Special Pleaders on both sides take up their cudgels to defend their positions so resolutely that neither hears the other in the resulting hullabaloo. That is their nature; for they must, above all, drown out, disregard, stop their ears against the case for the other side in their job-maintaining as in their ad-creating.

I must here repeat that I know of no other way for the advertising or promotion man to do his work other than to bury a large part of the truth. To do so was part of the contract he signed when he took the job. And, as he grows older, he becomes more expert at his burial operations until he has quite an investment in what he has learned about interring half the truth and presenting the other half most effectively. But that is so only of his trade. There is still all the rest of his life to consider.

A Possible, Passable Antidote

Every healthy worker knows that in his non-working hours it is best to reverse the conditions of his labor. The ditch digger ought to lazy around on his days off and drink beer. The clerk

ought to play golf or bowl and lift his voice in raucous rebellion against (and for contrast with) his careful behavior the rest of the week. The brain worker should dig in the garden or make ship models in bottles or play with his stamp collection. And the man who is paid to live and think and tell half-truths all his working life *would do well* to spend some of his spare time seeking out some whole truths and looking at them hard. For only in this way can he bring his life into balance and arrest the process of becoming just another Sweet Guy.

The healthy antidote to working hours spent in repeating, say, "My product is a perfect, shining thing," may well be leisure time passed in examining many things not merely whole but with the emphasis on the negative. To swing that pendulum somewhere back toward normal, it may be necessary for the ad man, as it was for me, to cultivate the delicious habit of fault-finding. It can provide the overdose of divine discontent required to counter all those thousands of working hours passed in adoring the affirmative. Consider, for example, just the seamy side of our environment.

Take private enterprise. It is, as most of us concede, the best way of life man has ever managed to evolve on this planet—but (as we almost never add) it stinks. Why *won't* we say it? Private enterprise is immensely superior to the managed systems of communism, fascism and other authoritarianisms. But on any scale of real excellence it scores hardly a passing grade. If 100 is perfection, perhaps communism gets a 5. And fascism another 5. But does private enterprise, the American Way, or whatever you want to call it, rate more than 25? All right, make it 50. It has not solved the problems of poverty or racial equality or security in illness or in age; it has sadly reduced the spiritual element in its society while overemphasizing the material; and it can't control its own technology (which threatens to blow it off the earth) or its rate of increase (which threatens to crowd it off). Private enterprise has a long way to go, and talking and thinking about it as if it were *your product and had no faults in it* is no part of your bargain with your employer or yourself.

Your Church, Your Social Life?

Get the picture of what I mean about fault-finding? It's marvelous therapy. Take your church, if you have one. It, too, probably has a long way to go from its present situation. Whatever it is and despite its many good works, doesn't it fail to fight the good fight for *unpopular* issues? Doesn't it persist in narrow bigotry toward other sects; doesn't it avoid facing up to the real problem in its parishioners' lives? I'll bet it does.

Your social life—let's look at *that*. Isn't it largely an extension of your office life—filled with hypocrisies in whose midst you try grandly to convince yourself that you're having a great time with a great gang doing the most exciting things? Hasn't your taste in art (if you ever had one) stopped developing; isn't your wife getting fat and sloppy; aren't the children too fresh, and where is their sense of excellence in anything? Take a long, negative look at the other side of the moon.

But when you do, beware. It will not make you a better company or agency advertising man. Just as your life work has been affecting your non-work life, once you begin seeing things in the round you're going to start losing your ability to see them only in the flat. So don't start this procedure too young—unless you want to change your job. Most men can't afford what I am suggesting until they're 45 or 50, but they can think about it and plan for it.

One of my favorite authors writes, "All is chaos, but a man can derive no satisfaction from chaos—and so a thoughtful man imposes on chaos an order of his own choosing and lives as if it were true." Yes, some of us finally reach a point where we want to choose our own order. We get tired of settling for one imposed on us by our self-supposed need to support a family better than it has any right to expect, or by our own compulsion to elbow our way up some pyramid to prove that we are so a man. In that event there are many courses to choose from.

And these choices have been made in many ways. I know a man who literally lives for East Orange, New Jersey. He has found truth in trying to reform his community—honestly and without cant. Another found the editorial half-truths of a national periodical too much for him (it's an editorial problem, too) and became an author. A sales director friend of mine gave it all up to become a Methodist minister, and a former research director I know is happily teaching sociology at Columbia. There is an ex-promotion man who quit to found a business in Lebanon, another who opened an appliance store and has built it into a chain. Each imposed on chaos an order of his own choosing, and is now living as if it is so.

There are other choices, of course. One is to hang on, accepting the half-truths and being gradually shoved aside or ignored until annuity time arrives. Another is to stay on and, if you are in a very powerful position, try to fight the system. But that takes a very tough hombre, for the Advertising Establishment is a business service and its faults are those of business—only, perhaps, more so. Educating any but the very superior businessman to the wiser use of advertising is like trying to turn a nearsighted person, interested only in today's profits, into a farsighted person, interested in protecting his investments and building for the long pull. Any oculist will tell you how difficult *that* is.

Meanwhile, as he waits for (and perhaps works toward) the attainment of that miracle, the advertising man is hoist by his own canard. Perhaps he likes it up there—but, if he does, he ought to be ashamed.

A few years ago, a survey sponsored by Advertising Age was made among the neighbors of ad men living in the suburbs of New York City, Chicago and Detroit. Among the findings were: Only 39 per cent would say "Fine" if a young man asked their advice about going into advertising . . . They agreed that advertising has the lowest prestige of six possible occupations including retailing . . . Only 2 per cent said the ad man was "Reliable, Responsible"; 53 per cent said he was "Neurotic" and "A Heavy Drinker"; and 59 per cent said he was "Glib and Superficial." Only 4 per cent would like their sisters to marry an ad man and only 4 per cent would like an ad man as a next-door neighbor, (7 per cent preferred "someone in retailing.")
—ADVERTISING AGE, *May 5, 1961*

DELUSION VIII

" *"Advertising doesn't need public relations"*

THE HUMAN PREDICAMENT along Madison Avenue takes many forms, and one that keeps reappearing may be stated thus: "How low will I stoop to win how much applause of the kind that I hate myself for wanting at all?"

This merry question sprang to mind once while I was reading the advertising column of one of New York's great dailies. It seems that the presidents of two of our major ad agencies were challenging a remark attributed by *Time* to the president of a third. For reasons we shall shortly explore, this gentleman had claimed that he plays the worst golf in the advertising business.

The statements of the challengers were unusual not only because they sprang from such Jovian lips but also for the vigor of the language in which they were couched. The entire foofaraw puzzled me. "Why," said I, "are these distinguished leaders of our profession vying for this dishonor so uproariously?" It quickly occurred to me that they deemed it no dishonor at all. On the contrary, they seemed to be doing a little public boasting. Under the guise of the phoniest kind of modesty, they were proclaiming their virtue to the world at large by implying that they have been too dedicated, or too busy all their lives mastering the tough trade of advertising, to have found the time to learn to play golf in any but the most awkward way.

Let us overlook, for a moment, the matter of taste in this tourney—the very delicate question of whether or not the chief executive officers of two of our largest ad agencies should permit themselves to be observed in public (this was *not* a trade paper) giggling over the right to carry away the jester's bladder. Would the simplest public relations major in any college or university (from which, ad men habitually complain, they are not able to attract the best and brightest minds) call this a spectacle of which their companies or their profession could be proud?

All the world wonders why advertising, the great image delineator, cannot project on the screen of our society something better than an unprepossessing, off-register blur of its own features. We may find a clue here—in this clownish act wherein two of advertising's most celebrated names stumble over one another to get mentioned cuddlesomely in a newspaper column.

The Shoemaker's Child Goes Barefoot

It is, in truth, just another piece of evidence that advertising has failed to understand that it desperately needs public relations to help it put its best foot forward (instead of the one that has just been muddied). It has had plenty of time to find this out—and plenty of wounds to show for its failure to do so. From the day long ago when the first consumer, fed up with the outrageous claims of the patent medicine advertisers, laid back his ears and bayed his indignation, it has been receiving unmistakable signals that it is in trouble. For patent medicine, read "deodorant" or any one of a hundred products sold today with a total absence of good taste that precipitates tons of protesting mail, hundreds of critical editorials and sermons, and oceans of ill will.

It is advertising's own blundering fault that the public does not understand it better. Advertising is, of course, one of the most

personal of all the economic forces brought to bear on the public. The more personal it is, the more dangerous it is to itself and the more effective it tends to be, until it flouts certain basic principles of good public relations; then it becomes suicidal. One would think that ad men would be aware of this and, therefore, nervously watchful of advertising's good manners and good name. But now that television has put the sight and sound of thousands of advertisements inside the consumer's living room, advertising is still putting the wrong feet forward with such regularity that you can hardly wonder that it is judged by the public first by how it irritates, annoys or disappoints and only then, if at all, by its manifold contributions to our life and time.

An Excellent Case for Itself

What can advertising do about this? Well, for one thing it might try to grow up and recognize a few facts of life. In 1712, the Tory government in Great Britain decided to tax periodical advertising partly because of the intemperate claims of the elixirs and patent medicines and partly as a rebuke to the Whig press. By the time they got around to repealing that tax and recovering from its effects, it was too late for Britain to become more than a Johnny-Come-Lately to the advertising scene, which the United States has dominated ever since.

It could happen here. Advertising can make an excellent case for itself; it has a good story to tell, but it is congenitally unable to agree on that story and make the story known. The case for advertising is a simple one—the self-evident right of a girl to be courted by as many men as want her. She has this right even

though every one of her suitors will put only his best foot forward, though none will tell her the whole truth about himself and though some will surely lie. Despite these expected corruptions of the truth, she should be permitted to see and hear all the evidence that the boys want to present, rather than to be handed over to any single groom like the purdahed bride of a Hindu family.

The assumption is that she knows men and is able to discount their boyish boasts and guess at the heinous sins behind their guilty silences. And out of the clamor of conflicting half-truths and evasions, she will be able, most times, to pick the best husband for herself.

There ought to be a way to say this so that it isn't too shameful a fall from the impossible summit of purity which advertising has been claiming for itself. But let advertising fail long enough to find that way and some deadly punitive measure like Britain's heavy tax may be the outcome.

The Foot-in-Mouth Disease

Consider, for example, the books on advertising by famous advertising men on which the public builds its image of the profession. They do little to ameliorate matters. But why are they so bad, so ludicrously bad? Because almost all of them are written to get business for the author or his ad agency—that's why. And because, consequently, they can't tell the truth about practically anything for fear of antagonizing practically everybody among the author's colleagues, clients and prospects—that's also why. In fact, no book on advertising written by an advertising agency executive while he is still actively engaged in getting and holding business for his agency is worth a tinker's dam—*without exception!* Most such books are nothing but overlong solicitations. And who knows better than an agency man that the man least qualified to write an ad is the man who makes the product or is responsible for the service to be advertised. If he wants a good ad written, he should retain a good advertising agency to do the job.

Of course, there are other reasons why so many famous, practicing ad men put their feet in their busy mouths every time they touch pencil to paper about their profession. Sometimes it's because they just can't write. (Not every good advertising man is a good copywriter.) Sometimes, although they can write, they have no taste. Sometimes they can write tastefully except about themselves (and then they titter or primp). Sometimes they're afraid they will give away their very own dear trade secrets—so afraid that they freeze up completely. And often, although they can make good ads, they don't know *how* they make them.

So why doesn't the knowledgeable ad man turn to the man most qualified to tell his story for him: the first-rate public relations man? Well, scattered attempts have been made in that direction but they have usually foundered on that old rock, human nature. A major reason for this lies in the difference between the two specialties. The kind of thinking required in advertising deals only with the market. The kind required in PR deals with the public, which is always bigger than and different from the market (yes, even in the case of Baby Ruth candy bars). PR concerns itself with any market only as it's an element in the larger group of which it is a part: all those millions who will never conceivably buy the product. And it does so on the very sound principle that this larger group, the public, the non-customers and non-prospects (editors, teachers, ministers and just plain gabby citizens), can create a reputation for a product that can either damage it in its market or give it the shine of popularity there. A management must, therefore, says PR, take the public into consideration in everything it does.

They Don't Like Each Other

The market and the public present two different kinds of problems, however, and it takes two different kinds of people using different approaches to manipulate them. So different are the approaches that it isn't hard to understand why ad men and PR men often have a difficult time getting along together. *The fact is that they hate each other's guts!*

This is especially true because one of their common denominators is the professional use of the printed word to achieve their ends. Wherever different kinds of writers foregather (poets with propagandists, newspaper men with writers of radio commercials, novelists with science popularizers), there the snot-green god of jealousy is present. You can see him clearly in advertising agencies that have their own PR departments. Here, the personnel dealing with product publicity poses no problems, for that phase of PR is only a little removed from advertising. The process is like ad writing except that the company is not going to pay for it and the odds are that the text will be reworded and condensed if it is ever printed at all.

But above the level of the publicity release the most savage kind of sibling rivalry begins to operate between the ad men and the PR people for the love of papa, the client. This is primarily because all the more important functions of PR involve the kind of decisions that only top management can make; many of them, in fact, are truly matters of business statesmanship. When, for example, the issue is how to minimize the impact on a great banking house of an abscondence with major company funds or the effect on a great airline of a tragic crash shown to be caused by negligence, only the president and the board chairman can work with the PR people. And when a corporation is trying to persuade Congress to pass a law that may mean billions to its future or is planning to do business (in seven figures) with a recognized but undeclared enemy of its government, the line executives are passed over and the working and thinking are all done in the top executive suite.

And while the PR men are working upstairs, the contacts of the ad men in most fields are limited to the advertising manager or, at the highest, the vice president in charge of marketing. When one realizes that advertising and public relations are generally conceded to be the two most status-conscious specialties in the business world, one is all too able to see why the little shades of patronage, the time spent with whom where and who sits highest at the table, are of overwhelming importance to the practitioners of both of these gray arts.

Revlon Is Not U.S. Steel

Of course, the matter of who wins is almost wholly a question in the long run of what industry is involved. At Revlon, for example, (or in any cosmetic firm) advertising is handled at the highest level and PR is a bad second except in emergency situations. But at U.S. Steel, advertising's contacts are several management steps below PR's. Where a major part of the firm's profits must go into advertising the advertising agency tends to get the top attention, as in the drug, cosmetic, cigarette, detergent and other consumer businesses. But where a smaller percentage goes into advertising and a larger amount of money and time is tied up in the labor situation, for example, or in some of the other legislative, scandalous or opportunistic situations I have already described, the PR man is firmly in the catbird seat.

A Peck of Pickled Peepers

But what is this pecking order of which we speak—this shifting, slipping system of values in which first the PR man and then the ad man is patted on the head or told to cool his heels? It is not merely a matter of those two ancient rivals, the Ben Sonnenbergs and the David Ogilvys. There are pecking orders within pecking orders. Inside public relations there are levels of reward and respect building upward from the lowly, aforementioned writer of releases to that confidant of kings, the master business statesman. And on the advertising side we have, of course, a similar situation, ranging from the copy cub or flap artist to the $60,000-a-year creative director, with all the grades in between, jockeying like mad to better their positions.

It is true that in the combined firmament containing both the advertising and PR worlds, the writer of publicity releases occupies the coldest and most barren planet furthest from the sun, the clinker in outer space. This is because nothing he writes is expected to appear in print the way he writes it; he is the asker of alms, scratching at the gate. Unlike the advertisement writer, he hasn't the price of admission for his copy.

By contrast, that statesmanlike fellow we described earlier in this chapter—that schemer of grandiose schemes, that groomer and stager of men who lures the editors into making his client their "Man of the Year" (not by bribing them but by handling his man so skillfully that he appears to deserve the lofty title), *he* is on a great, shining planet near the sun—no nearer than advertising's, mind you, but a very favored one. Such an artisan ranks way up in the hierarchy—he speaks but to papa and the chairman of the board.

Call Girls and Retroactive Prophecy

Well, who and what is this PR paragon? Anyone may be excused for not knowing, because more nonsense has been written and said about the sprawling domain of modern public relations than even about the advertising business. If you read the newspapers, you might think that everybody and anybody was in PR today. A famous Negro, whose business is prize fighting, turns up on page one as a PR man for Fidel Castro's Cuba. A gorgeous redheaded call girl picked up by the cops prettily tells them she's "in publicity." Home run sluggers parlaying their profits and national renown into starting a bowling alley suddenly blossom into fullblown "publicists" to shill their new sideline. In fact, it's become quite fashionable, especially if you're out of work, to say that you're "in PR."

There are parallels galore throughout history for almost every phase of modern PR, but those of us who were around in the depressed '30's know that the PR of today took a giant step forward right there. It really got itself organized in those lean days, and the reason was that business was scared. You would have been, too, if people were running around calling you a "merchant of death" and a great national figure was promising to "drive the money-changers from their temples." It was then that business discovered semantics. Businessmen found that although they could talk a great game, nobody seemed to be listening. To get their hearing they had to turn to the PR man who knew how it was done.

"Sez You!" Said the Public

Note that business did not turn to advertising for help in that critical time. The ad man could do no more than write his client's message and get it printed in a paid ad which the public would not quite believe. "Sez *you!*" the public sez, reading an ad about how public-spirited a company is, signed and paid for by said company. But the PR man knew how to put that message in words and forms that an editor might accept—thus giving it the credibility of an independent respected spokesman. In other words, the PR man knew how to write a certain kind of factual-sounding persuasion that the ad man could not produce. It had the sound of the whole truth, although it practically never was, and the PR man, having probably been at one time a newspaper man, knew how to achieve that fine, balanced-seeming, objective tone better than any other writer—especially better than the ad writer, who had never tried to sound as if he was more than a special pleader.

It is an interesting fact that you can scarcely get to first base in business today without committing yourself to paper. That so many executives do it so poorly could well be a prime reason for that shrinking net profit they're forever grousing about. Dull, wordy, obscure copy goes in and comes out of business offices in fantastic quantities; it is a criminal waste of everyone's time. And yet, no business can operate without written communication among all its interior departments and the outside world.

Thousands of executives who can speak, read and hear the English language with relative efficiency seem to be blind to the form it must take to communicate its meaning on paper. They do not know the mechanics and techniques of writing, and so they can neither do it themselves nor appraise good writing when it is put in front of them. And one of the main reasons for that is they don't read enough good writing.

Are You Undergeneralized?

I happen to believe that the man who allows himself to become under-read is characterized by a certain immaturity. I also believe that men who are under-read tend both to oversimplify and to be undergeneralized—and that the undergeneralized man is a case of arrested development. Notice that I didn't say over-specialized, for we need specialists in our increasingly complex society. Chairman Floyd Bond, of Pomona College's economics department, puts it very well when he says: "What we want is not lawyers, but men practicing law, not doctors, but men practicing medicine. For a good society, we must have not specialists and broad-gauge people, but specialists who *are* broad-gauge people." And, I might add, businessmen who are also communicators.

The problem of semantics wasn't the only problem that business had to face during the period when its very foundations were being questioned by an angry public in the grim Thirties. It found that one unfavorable piece of legislation resulting from the pressures of public opinion could put a score of companies out of business. Exhibit A was the Public Utility Holding Company Act, which did just that. In other words, business discovered that its profitability was critically dependent upon the opinions of those who produced, supplied, distributed, bought and used its goods and services, and that it had better mend its ways with them. That meant adopting the policy of "social responsibility" which Edward L. Bernays, one of the earliest and best of the PR men, had been advocating for years. Today PR's main endeavor is to create a sense of "social responsibility" in its clients— a job it has done well in some fields, but not in advertising.

Advertising is presently taking a second look at PR. It does not see much status in it: the first big corporation president is still to arrive via the PR route. And not enough money has been made in PR to excite the ad man. (PR has had a hard time figuring out how to charge for its myriad services.)

But things are changing. According to *Business Week*, PR is now a $2 billion-a-year business in the U.S.—one-sixth the size of advertising, and growing faster than advertising. Whereas not one in fifty of the nation's biggest corporations had full-fledged PR departments in 1936, three out of four have them now and thousands of other companies employ fulltime consultants. "By almost any yardstick," says *Business Week*, "its growth has been spectacular." Furthermore, PR now has power. It alone has saved some businesses in trouble from going under. And no matter what newspaper men say (their gripes are mainly over stupid or phony copy by incompetents, of which PR has plenty), few if any media would have the staff and resources to cover business news were it not for PR.

Fuzz in the Back of the Bus

Nevertheless, the average ad man still feels secure enough to regard all this with an elder's condescension. One such, a Chicago ad agency copy supervisor, even took it upon himself recently to straighten the PR man out in an issue of his own *Public Relations Journal*. His thesis was that "public relations has become underprivileged and is losing by default," and he offered to tell it "How to Get Out of the Back of the Bus."

"A few years ago," he said, "we were all in the back of the bus. But the important thing is that the advertising people have moved up front, and, to these eyes, the public relations people have not." "That's because PR's image is 'fuzzy,'" the man said, "and not as prestigious or as authoritative or as definite as that of the advertising agency."

"When a client wants advice on how to plan and coordinate the distribution efforts of his company's products," the ad man gurgled, "he is not interested in talking to an ex-newspaperman!"

Perhaps not, but let the client get involved in a proxy fight that may cost him his company, or a costly labor dispute, or let him see Congressional legislation of the kind threatening the insurance and drug industries loom on *his* horizon, and hear him holler for—the ad man? Heavens to Betsy, no!—he hollers for that feeble, pitiful "ex-newspaperman" he's not interested in talking to.

That bus the Chicagoan is riding up front in may well need a new set of windshield wipers. For it is the increasing effectiveness of PR in promoting the sales of products and services that has moved advertising to take a second look at it. PR is and has been mainly concerned with selling the business enterprise itself, not its products and services, but the findings of the social scientists regarding what makes consumers buy and not buy is altering that. They do or don't buy, it seems, for an infinitude of reasons, many of them not susceptible to advertising's frontal attack. But they *may* be susceptible to PR's oblique attack on the attitudes and beliefs that form the climate of opinion in which the advertising message must sink or swim. Nobody knows for sure, but PR has been making pilot attacks—with some success.

There is further grist for advertising's second look in a recent questioning of 205 manufacturers by the National Industrial Conference Board regarding their opinion of PR. The spectrum of these companies ranged from largest to smallest, and more than 80 per cent of them had their own PR departments or employed outside counsel. What they had to say was not all favorable to PR ("far from a clear-cut function," "hard to measure," etc.), but they voted for the *credibility* attached to information about them conveyed through PR. And the president of a large industrial machinery firm said, "A favorable story in a trade magazine, for example, carries far more persuasiveness than an equivalent-sized advertisement. And we have found it far less costly."

It is true that PR's image is, as the ad man claims, "fuzzy," but why shouldn't it be when it is involved in almost everything from building up a Hollywood ingenue named, say, Tuesday Wednesday (that's press agentry) to promoting a product called, say, "Frog-Off" (that's publicity) to mounting a campaign against featherbedding for the railroads whose foreseen destiny is a U. S. Supreme Court ruling (that's public relations). The passage of time will no doubt resolve the fuzz on PR's image; meanwhile, trying to define it is pointless. "It is," as Harry Carlson, one of PR's better practitioners, says, "like frisking a seal—you don't come up with much."

Advertising's image has just as much fuzz on it: direct mail,

mail order, institutional, image-building, television, billboard—
"Where it will all end" (as *The New Yorker* once said of *Time*)
"knows God." And advertising is in trouble while PR isn't. I am
not at all certain that even the proper use of PR could alter the
climate of opinion advertising has created for itself and must
now live with. It is indeed stuck with the half-truth, which is
its bread and butter, and with the sins and excesses of a minority
of its members who have diminished that half-truth to a quarter-
truth, a tenth-truth or no-truth-at-all. It needs PR, all right, for at
least PR tries to make its stories sound like the whole truth—
enough so, at any rate, to fool its audience which (we must remember) is practically never the public or the market. The audience of PR is a relatively small number of what Edward L.
Bernays habitually calls "incipient foci of benevolent infection"
—by which he means the editors, clergymen, teachers and more
influential members of our society who talk a lot and write a lot
and influence a lot of people. PR pays this audience the compli-
ment of seeming to keep up appearances; it is often plausible if
never dispassionate. It "massages these foci," as Bernays puts it—
with a fine contempt for the unmixed metaphor. PR does not,
cynically, gear itself to its most moronic target, imposing over-
simplifications of bloodstreams absorbing pain-killers, in diagrams
so patently faked that even a bright ten-year-old must exclaim,
"Baloney!" It spares its audience the "Nasometer Test" and those
impossible shampoo transformations that turn a shaggy bitch into
a svelte charmer in one sudsing. PR at least *pretends* to be a true
account (a "newspaper story"), and that is decent of it, so decent that, compared with advertising's cynical stupidities, PR looks
almost like a gentleman.

Ivan in the Gray Flannel Suit

Perhaps one of the most interesting things that can be said about
advertising at the moment is that the Russians, after denouncing it
for years as vulgar and wasteful, have begun to copy it. They have,
for some time, been running help-wanted and classified ads as well
as public announcements whenever certain products are, despite
state planning, in over-supply. Very recently, in Moscow, they
have been interviewing representatives of a large publishing house

with magazines circulating throughout Europe, Asia, Africa and South America. It is said that they have some sort of image-building or image-changing campaign in mind. Although the appearance of such advertising in the United States is not, at the moment, believed to be under consideration, the day may not be far away. One can imagine the reactions of Birchers and other Red-baiters upon finding a color spread in *Life* or the *Saturday Evening Post* headlined "Are Your Ideas About Russia Out of Date" and showing Uncle Sam shaking hands with Uncle Ivan across the Atlantic while the Man in the Moon smiles benignly upon them both.

Whatever its faults and its future, however, advertising is now an essential part of the distribution system that has made mass production and the U. S. standard of living possible. In fact, it is a form of vulgar and wasteful free speech in our free society, and it has a fundamental right to be seen and heard, special pleader though it may be. It has standards no higher than those of the five men vying for the heiress' hand, or of any ten men applying for a desirable job, half-truthing, exaggerating and often lying its way into markets it doesn't deserve. It is, in short, no better than its host, Private Enterprise, which, as I have said, may be a lousy way of running an economy but is still the best that we have come up with.

And so, let advertising seduce, says the author—and let it take the consequences. Any attempt by taxation to cripple it or the media it sustains would probably repeat the even greater folly that Britain has had to undo.

But perhaps it *is* time for advertising to stop knocking PR and to learn how to use it. PR is getting richer and more powerful and is looking toward the day when it can afford to buy or start ad agencies of its own. That would make advertising an arm of PR, which may well be its destiny. For if it came to a showdown between the half-truths of advertising and the fake whole truths of PR, the phony whole truth might prove more acceptable to the greater number. And then we would witness the ultimate absurdity in this curious charade—the spectacle of the crooked tail waving half a dog!

It is a corollary of the free market that no supplier can be blamed for meeting a demand. If, as in the sale of narcotics, so doing is against the public welfare, it is the government's duty to make the satisfaction of the demand illegal and to frustrate such satisfaction. But, until that time, the supplier is blameless.

DELUSION IX

"The shortcomings of advertising are the fault of the advertising men"

THE CHIEF WAY in which advertising deludes business is by permitting or even encouraging businessmen to believe certain things about advertising *which simply are not true.*

Its purpose in doing so is always the same: to get or hold a client, to retain or increase income.

Because very little about the way in which advertising accomplishes its ends is conclusively demonstrable, it is easy to encourage a businessman in his beliefs about the way advertising works, even though those beliefs are based on irrelevant or nonexistent facts and forces.

Thus, when vice-president-for-marketing B takes over the job from vice-president-for-marketing A and wants to discredit his predecessor, he may state forcefully and without evidence that A has been wasting the firm's money by putting 75 per cent of its advertising dollars into daytime radio. At this point the advertising agency can either discover suddenly that vice president B has an astonishing and hitherto unsuspected talent for advertising or look for another account. For, as inevitably as the fact that the highest billing goes to the most skillful yea-sayer, another agency will come forward with indisputable proof that B is right if the reigning agency refuses to do so.

The situation (and it arises continuously) always reminds me of a "Sweetie-Pie" cartoon in which a large dog is shown standing at point. The savage girl-child who is the heroine of the piece has obviously done something very wrong and the dog is pointing out her hiding place to the moppet's mother. Says Sweetie-Pie

between clenched teeth,
"When you were learning
to point I hope
you also took lessons on how to open
your own cans of dog food."

Who stoopeth lowest to concur
Will loudest hear the client's purr;
But he who flouts the client's wish
Will sup from cracked and empty dish.

Side by side with the truism that a successful agency must hoe its own row (seeming, if possible, not to be doing so), stands another unpleasant fact. One of the great truisms of trade is that no manufacturer with a successful business improves his product *at increased cost* except under the strongest pressure. The exception, of course, is the erratic and rare altruist who, having tasted all flavors except that of righteousness, confuses business with philanthropy and decides that come-willy, come-nilly, he will make his Thingums the best damned Thingums that anyone will ever see. After his company goes bankrupt, he sits by the side of the road and benignly watches the world go by. Aside from this lunatic (or saint), the rest of business reacts to any suggestion that it increase costs to improve its product only with the most savage resistance and yields only to the most unremitting and powerful pressure. This pressure may be immediate or anticipated. It can be brought to bear on the manufacturer by his customers (who may exercise it by stepping down their purchases for lack of the improvement); or by his competitors (who may supply the needed improvement and thus take his customers away from him); or by his government (which may make selling his product without the improvement unlawful). But, without such pressures, there will be no improvement year after year. In fact, a case may be made that any manager who manufactures a product or renders a service more expensively than he must in order to maintain a maximum sale at a maximum profit is guilty of depriving the stockholders of income.

"And What Have WE to Do with Excellence?"

The New York *Herald Tribune* reported in February, 1965, that Rep. Oren Harris, D., Ark., chairman of the House Commerce Committee and one of Congress' chief watchdogs over broadcasting, had suggested that the commercial television networks and stations should not be expected to be creators of excellence in cultural programming. As reported in the *Herald Tribune,* Rep. Harris felt that such cultural escalation was not the function of the broadcasters and that the Communications Act freed broadcasters from responsibility for cultural and "artistic" programming.

Said Harris, the networks and stations, sponsors and their agencies "do not and cannot offer opportunities for excellence in cultural program categories," but he did not see this as ground for criticizing them. "It is merely a frank recognition of the diversity of man's talents, temperaments and aims," he said. "We do not criticize birds for not being able to swim. . . . We should not blame commercial organizations for not being versatile enough to provide adequate opportunities for excellence in cultural and artistic programming."

The truth is that an advertiser can get advertising that is just as good as he wants, if he is willing to pay for it. But what he must pay is not only (or even most importantly) money; too often it is time, and lots of it. True, the better advertising agencies preparing, let us assume, better advertising, are less likely to make deals involving rebates on commissions or fee-cutting. And to this extent, better advertising costs the advertiser more money. But dollars won't do it by themselves. Someone in top management must be continuously, knowledgeably and aggressively interested in the firm's advertising if it is ever going to be more than merely adequate. And that is where we come into headlong collision with the Law of Symbiotic Relationships which says that

parasites will seek out the host that derives profit from them and protects them, regardless of the host's relative unimportance in the larger scheme. Thus, left to itself, an advertising agency will produce the advertising most likely to win the approval of the most powerful officer in the client organization who is willing to put up a fight when someone suggests that the agency be fired. That official may be a relative nobody and probably will be—for the somebodies are usually more interested in production or engineering or financing than in advertising. The nobody chosen as host may very well want to use the firm's advertising to forward his own personal career, and that is the kind of advertising he will get, if he won't bother (as, mostly, he won't) to think about and learn about his advertising problems as a professional ad man would.

"Make Me Make It Better, Please"

The businessman buying his advertising for ulterior purposes or entrusting it to stupes is no more guilty of venality or negligence than others.

There are so many parallels to the proposition that no one improves his product until he is forced to that you can almost name an industry at random and find the condition existing there in its fullest (or rankest) flowering.

Planes and automobiles? Who will deny that they can be made both safer and sturdier than they are now? And what maker will do so until forced by the market, the competition or the government?

Foods? Those lethal winding-key coffee cans are finally out, one hears, watching the boys tear off the tops of their beer cans. The increasing sale of bread that tastes like bread is beginning to make the big bakeries think hard about reforming their sponge-rubber products. The pear people have discovered that it pays to sell ripe fruit instead of green fruit allowed to rot a little on the way to market. Maybe melons will be next and perhaps even tree-sweetened if un-dyed oranges may appear on the market.

The fountain pen industry is a dead industry today, killed by ballpoints and the Japanese brush pens. It refused to see the writing on the wall even after the competition was scribbling the news in increased sales all over the Western world.

But let us return to advertising. I said that the businessman buying his advertising is no more guilty of venality or negligence than most. People buy cars and homes and foreign travel, refrigerators, burial plots and television sets with little or no knowledge of what they are getting. It cannot surprise anyone but the most innocent that the advertising industry fails to improve its products when nobody seems to care whether he gets his money's worth of anything! The wonder is not that things are so shoddy and services so slipshod but that they are even as good as they are.

Why should the advertising man prepare better ads? Who demands it? The advertiser? The consumer? The government? None of these three—although all keep up a perpetual, querulous keening about raising standards and creating codes. But not enough advertisers refuse to buy bad advertising—not enough consumers refuse to buy badly advertised products—and government does not insist with nearly enough muscle that advertising improve itself to bring about a change.

The attitude of the tire industry toward its responsibility to improve its product is all too relevant here. It, too, passes the buck to its customers—but in terms franker than those usually used when government threatens to step in and regulate.

For some time there have been rumors that the Federal Trade Commission may propose to the Commerce Department that the government's minimum safety requirements for auto and truck tires (set by the National Bureau of Standards in 1952) be revised drastically to accommodate the new and swifter highway speeds and heavier loading habits that have developed over the past decade. *The New Republic,* in its issue of January 30, 1965, observes that, "Mr. John F. Floberg, secretary and general counsel for Firestone, was undoubtedly reflecting a good deal of the industry's feeling when he declared: 'Probably the worst thing the Commission could do from the standpoint of customer protection would be to attempt to establish grades of quality, as has sometimes been suggested, on the basis of physically measurable dimensions or mathematically countable characteristics . . . I submit that the best standard, the time-tested and proved standard and the appropriate free enterprise standard of quality should be the one that has in the case of tires, as in the case of other consumer products, worked most satisfactorily; namely, *the discriminating and sophisticated taste of the American consumer.' "*

A Taste for Self-Destruction

This "discriminating and sophisticated taste" of which Mr. Floberg speaks so admiringly, doesn't seem to work to the advantage of its owners in a great many fields including foods, drugs, liquors and (most recently) cigarettes. In fact, it seems to operate so murderously in anything that may harm the American consumer that he might well be considered to be hell-bent on his own destruction, a national suicide that has been frustrated only by his government stepping in again and again to prevent his being bilked, poisoned or smashed to bits by his own good taste.

Despite its protests, the tire industry seems blandly to recognize the inevitability of government supervision by passing the buck on to its customers in the traditional American way with the traditional phrase that always precedes regulation from Washington: "We only give them guys what they want." That is everybody's plea—from the old complaints of Hollywood before the movies got themselves regulated (too late) to the righteousness of Detroit (disciplined a few years back, not by government but by foreign competition) when the public rebelled against the chromium monsters.

It should be noted that advertising's customers are not the consumers of advertised products but *the consumers of advertising*—the businessmen of America. And when advertising passes the buck to *its* customers, it is only doing what the rest of the boys do and what the system actually seems to have been set up to have done.

Self-regulation has never been effective in anything from personal evacuation to international trade. The best to be expected is that man will keep a jump ahead of the sheriff, and only the preternaturally wise man manages to do even that. Will private medicine, for example, continue eking out its little reluctant concessions to the underprivileged with enough skill and foresight to keep that step ahead of socialized medicine? Perhaps. But it will be a very close thing. And certainly private medicine would be nowhere in its turtle-paced program to help the needy if it had not been prodded by the do-gooders and the government.

Wanted—a Powerful Nudger

Who will prod advertising enough to force it to do the things it should and stop doing what it shouldn't? The businessman ought to wield the trident—he has the most at stake. But to do so he must learn something about advertising, a great deal more than he now knows. It isn't enough for him to spend his money; he must learn to spend it wisely and it is my guess that *he will not take the trouble.*

It is a horrifying fact that the public has never taken the trouble to learn enough about medicine (where its very life is at stake) to select its doctors for anything but their personality or its hospitals on any basis except groundless trust in groups of men who too frequently have political and financial axes to grind. The doctors don't regulate themselves, the public reneges and, sad to say, that leaves only the government. Or is it "sad to say"? Perhaps that's what a government is for.*

The fact is that none of the broad justifications for advertising's existence has ever quite satisfied me.

The conventional claim that advertising creates mass demand and is therefore the cause of lower prices leaves me elaborately unconvinced. Sometimes the savings of mass production are passed on to the consumer and sometimes they are not: it's a naughty world. And increased demand doesn't always bring in its wake reductions in production costs great enough to offset the cost of advertising. Who knows, overall, what the great score is?

Advertising's claim to usefulness as a means of communication seems more valid provided we all admit that the communication is, as I have said, but a half-truth in which only that part which is to the advantage of the seller is presented. (At its worst, of

---

* As an advertising man, I should be free in my mind to scheme the most seductive schemes possible to get people to buy my product while, as a citizen, I should know that my government is policing me and my kind, preventing me from telling untruths that can injure the public in demonstrable ways. If I don't have to worry about policing myself, I can produce much better seductions. And if the government doesn't have to worry about cuddling up to the ANA or the AAAA or any other business interest and openly acts as a policeman protecting the public, it can do a better job of policing. For example, in June of 1965, a revolutionary court decision in a case initiated by the government held that the advertising agency responsible for the public bamboozlement reported on page 96 was legally responsible for presenting misleading or false claims for its client's products, even if based on the client's research. The agency was judged liable to the tune of a $50,000 fine. The client, Regimen, was fined some $53,000 and its president another $50,000 and sent to jail. There's a lot of dirty pool going on, but every now and then the ball goes into the right pocket. Only, however, when someone shoots straight. And who is better qualified to wield the cue in cases like these than our own Uncle Sam?

course, it is a series of outright lies whose authors are sometimes but not always discovered and punished.) There are other apologia, but these, too, seem equivocal.

Recently, however, I have found a justification I can live with. I touched upon it briefly in a preceding chapter, and I pass it on here to those readers who, as I do, like to worry this sort of un-nourishing bone. *The justification for advertising is the justification for free speech, even lying free speech.* Not only has a man got the right to lie as much as he wants as long as he doesn't harm anyone; it's his bounden duty to lie about himself, his product and his exploits. How else would he get himself married, his product sold, himself noticed in a world where everyone is lying? Or half-lying.

From the consumer's point of view, the justification for advertising is that of the attractive girl who demands the right to hear all her suitors so she can choose among them instead of having a husband selected for her as in the bad, old days. All are lying; she knows that. None will tell her the whole truth about himself; his person, his family, his connections, his prospects, his prejudices. There will be the real phony in whose braggadocio there will be no truth at all. There will be the sly and careful suitor who claims that he is and has much more than he has the right to claim, but will never exactly lie about it. And there will be the solid guy, the best of the lot, the best anyone has a right to ex-

pect, who will tell only the truth about himself, although even he will "put his best foot forward"—meaning that he will conceal his worse foot and fail to mention his Aunt Griselda (who died insane), or his foul temper when crossed, or the fact that his job is a little shaky, or that he isn't at all sure he wants "just slews of children."

The bride-to-be will hear them all and choose one from among them; that is her right. But her name is legion and her judgment ranges from superhuman to submoronic, her urge from self-expression to self-immolation. And so her subconscious will often choose the braggart, the phony, just as the consumer often selects the meretricious, showy product that won't stand up and is overpriced. In fact, come to think of it, every purchase tells us something about the buyer: about her character, personality and her needs beyond the obvious ones. By their shopping lists shall we know them. It may well be that the purchases of Americans, like their marriages, are made (not on Madison Avenue) but in heaven.

And thus do the brands exercise their free speech and the consumers exercise their free choice, and out of the resulting pandemonium emerges the free market.

Somehow, it all sounds too neat and foreordained, doesn't it? Like a delusion. Perhaps it is.

All men give three things to life in return for a living: their energy, their brains and their self-respect. Their only choice is how they will mix the ingredients—and even this is limited by the caprice of destiny which distributes two of the three most unevenly.

But you, I beg you, check your rage and scorn.
For man needs help from every creature born.
                    —BERTOLT BRECHT

DRAMATIS PERSONAE

WHAT is the cast of characters in the tragicomedy that this book has been discussing? For better or for worse, who are the makers and shakers of this world—not just the ones who move it with power or money but also those who brake it against progress or offer it largely unheeded wisdom or are merely the cleverist (if also the most superficial)?

Oddly enough, such a list was not to be found when the author sought it—unless he was willing to settle for the too inclusive memberships of the American Association of Advertising Agencies and the Association of National Advertisers (about three thousand individuals in all). The fact is that the few hundred really outstanding men and women of advertising don't seem to get much personal visibility in the general U.S. business community.

And so, implying neither praise nor blame, including influences both satanic and celestial (and making his selection only on the grounds that these people seem to be having the most effect on advertising as this book goes to press), the author here presents a very personal "Dramatis Personae of Advertising" . . .

Jack Gould, *New York Times*
Harry L. Hicks, Jr., Hicks & Greist
John H. Hoefer, Hoefer, Dieterich & Brown
Charles Feldman, Young & Rubicam
Charles S. Winston, Jr., Foote, Cone & Belding
F. William Free, McCann-Marschalk Co.
D. H. Echols, Fuller & Smith & Ross
Walter Weir, West, Weir & Bartel
Lawrence Valenstein, Grey Advertising
Robert W. Robb, Reach, McClinton & Co.

Walter Guild, Dance-Fitzgerald-Sample Co.
Edward N. Ney, Young & Rubicam
Jerome B. Gray, Gray & Rogers
Morris Hite, Tracy-Locke Co.
Richard Tobin, *Saturday Review*
William B. Murphy, Campbell Soup
Julian Koenig, Papert, Koenig, Lois
C. B. Ryan, Firestone
Curtis Berrien, Needham, Harper & Steers
David J. Mahoney, Colgate Palmolive

G. Montagu Miller, Kelly, Nason
John McGinty, Ralston Purina
S. Heagan Bayles, Sullivan, Stauffer, Colwell & Bayles
M. Crawford Pollock, Green Giant
Will C. Grant, Grant Advertising
Esther Peterson
David B. Arnold, Gray & Rogers
Paul Sheldon, Gulf Oil
Ernest A. Jones, MacManus, John & Adams
Carl Rogers, *Madison Avenue*
Robert E. Healy, The Interpublic Group of Companies
Ward F. Parker, Beechnut-Life Savers
James P. Wilkerson, Young & Rubicam
Ernest Zobian, Vick Chemical
H. W. Cooper, Meldrum and Fewsmith
Ross Millhiser, Philip Morris
Donald P. Nathanson, North Advertising
Milton F. Harrington, Liggett & Myers
William D. Laurie, Jr., J. Walter Thompson Co.
John Burgard, Brown & Williamson
Rudolph Montgelas, Ted Bates & Co.
Lawrence W. Bruff, Liggett & Myers
Barton A. Cummings, Compton Advertising
James A. Gordon, H.J. Heinz
Philip H. Schaff, Jr., Leo Burnett Co.
Paul Lohmeyer, Carling Brewing
Daniel S. Karsch, Daniel & Charles
Howard Gossage
Leo Burnett, Leo Burnett Co.
Victor Elting, Quaker Oats
Bernard P. Gallagher
Robert Farrell, Monsanto
Fred Adams, G. M. Basford Co.
Kenneth L. Skillin, Armour
Alan M. Ward, BBD & O
John H. Childs, Texaco
George H. Weber, Cole & Weber
John B. Hunter, B. F. Goodrich
Kenneth R. Oelschlager, Campbell-Mithun
J. D. Elgin, Socony Mobil
Ray Mithun, Campbell-Mithun
J. G. Smale, Procter & Gamble
Fred W. Adams, American Motors
Arthur Murphy, McCall Corp.
Floyd Hall, Eastern Airlines
Franklin E. Schaffer, Doremus & Co.
R. A. Davis, National Dairy
Robert Gage, Doyle Dane Bernbach
Margaret Hockaday, Hockaday Associates
Charles R. Standen, Tatham-Laird & Kudner
Judson H. Irish, Foote, Cone & Belding
Steve Frankfurt, Young & Rubicam
A. E. Duram, Fuller & Smith & Ross
Chester L. Posey, McCann-Erickson
Robert Betts, William Esty Co.
David B. McCall, C. J. LaRoche & Co.
Charles Farran, Griswold-Eshleman Co.
Charles E. Jones, Potts-Woodbury
Robert F. Carney, Foote, Cone & Belding
Dermott F. McCarthy, Young & Rubicam
R. B. Walker, American Tobacco
William W. Neal, Liller Neal Battle & Lindsey
William Wrigley, Wrigley
Clifford D. Field, Ogilvy, Benson & Mather

George Mosley, Seagram
W. Stanley Redpath, Ketchum, MacLeod & Grove
James E. Burke, Johnson & Johnson
Jeremy Gury, Ted Bates & Co.
Rex Budd, Campbell Soup
Wilson A. Shelton, Compton Advertising
Donald Frey, Ford
Donald Tennant, Leo Burnett Co.
Thomas C. Law, Jr., Coca-Cola
Leonard H. Lavin, Alberto Culver
Robert M. Ganger, D'Arcy Advertising Co.
Robert M. Gray, Humble Oil
Morris E. Jacobs, Bozell & Jacobs
Farish Jenkins, National Biscuit
Thomas C. Dillon, BBD & O
R. A. Uihlein, Schlitz
Neal W. O'Connor, N. W. Ayer & Son
E. W. Ebel, General Foods
David Botsford, Jr., Botsford, Constantine & Gardner
Martin Kaiden, *Business Week*
James M. Wallace, N. W. Ayer & Son
Henry Hunter, Olin Matthieson
Warner S. Shelly, N. W. Ayer & Son
J. R. Barlow, Chrysler
Carl W. Nichols, Jr., Cunningham & Walsh
Robert K. Heimann, American Tobacco
Ben Sonnenberg
Kenneth B. Arrington, Continental Baking
Edward Miller, Politz
F. E. Benson, Canada Dry
Milton Mayer
James Bowling, Philip Morris
Dan Whitney, Whitney & Whitney
Joseph Kaselow, New York *Herald Tribune*
Rolland W. Taylor, Foote, Cone & Belding
Charles V. Skoog, Jr., Hicks & Greist
Louis Honig, Honig-Cooper & Harrington
D. C. Stewart, Kenyon & Eckhardt
Clinton E. Frank, Clinton E. Frank
Charles L. Rumrill, Rumrill Co.
Charles E. Claggett, Gardner Advertising Co.
John P. Warwick, Warwick & Legler
Arthur C. Fatt, Grey Advertising
Lester Leber, Leber Katz Paccione
Milton Goodman, Gumbinner-North Co.
Norman B. Norman, Norman, Craig & Kummel
W. Walter Watts, RCA
Edward T. Parrack, Ketchum, MacLeod & Grove
Robert J. Piggott, Pet Milk
Frederic Papert, Papert, Koenig, Lois
Michael P. Ryan, Allied Chemical
Paul C. Harper, Jr., Needham, Harper & Steers
Thomas B. McFadden, TWA
Kenneth Laird, Tatham-Laird & Kudner
Wrigley Offield, Wm. Wrigley Jr. Co.
David Ogilvy, Ogilvy, Benson & Mather
H. L. Reed, AT&T
Fairfax M. Cone, Foote, Cone & Belding
Edward S. McKay, GE
William Bernbach, Doyle Dane Bernbach
J. R. McMenamin, US Rubber
David G. Watrous, Earle Ludgin & Co.
W. O. Maxwell, International Harvester
Marion Harper, Jr., The Interpublic Group of Companies

Ben Wells, 7-Up
William J. Colihan, Jr., Young & Rubicam
J. B. Williams, Kimberley-Clark
Christopher W. Cross, Post-Keyes-Gardner
C. W. Moodie, Armstrong Cork
Richard Bowman, Norman, Craig & Kummel
Daniel Ladd, P. Lorillard
Adolph J. Toigo, Lennen & Newell
Fred W. Dickson, Coca-Cola
Clarence Hatch, Jr., Campbell-Ewald Co.
James Fish, General Mills
Leon Morgan, Buchen Advertising
Robert E. Gorman, Allstate Insurance
Howard W. Chalk, Altman, Stoller, Chalk Adv.
Harriet Van Horne, *World-Telegram & Sun*
Charles Goldschmidt, Daniel & Charles
Eugene F. Loveland, Shell Oil
Norman B. Foster, Barnes Chase/Advertising
J. P. Kelley, Goodyear
Charles H. Brower, BBD & O
Donald Kendall, Pepsi Cola
Richard A. R. Pinkham, Ted Bates & Co.
C. C. Hollister, IBM
Albert R. Whitman, Campbell-Mithun
Myers B. Cather, Bristol Myers
Wallace L. Shepardson, Chirurg & Cairns
Leslie C. Bruce, Purex
Whitman Hobbs, Benton & Bowles
John E. Grimm III, Colgate Palmolive
Kensinger Jones, Campbell-Ewald Co.
Gail Smith, General Motors
Roger M. Kirk, Jr., Lehn & Fink
John P. Kennedy, Bristol Myers
Richardson Wood, Consultant in Research
Harold J. Beeby, Miles Labs.
Ted Callis, *Wall Street Journal*
Ralston Coffin, RCA
Kai Jorgensen, Hixson & Jorgensen
Marvin Corwin, Erwin Wasey, Ruthrauff & Ryan
Norman H. Strouse, J. Walter Thompson Co.
Shepard Kurnit, Delehanty, Kurnit & Geller
Stephens Dietz, Kenyon & Eckhardt
R. E. Allen, Fuller & Smith & Ross
Alfred J. Seaman, Sullivan, Stauffer, Colwell & Bayles
John H. Peace, William Esty Co.
Lee King, Edward H. Weiss and Co.
E. L. Deckinger, Grey Advertising
W. T. Okie, J. M. Mathes
William Strosahl, William Esty Co.
Judd Pollock, MPO Videotronics
Charles Revson, Revlon
Rosser Reeves, Ted Bates & Co.
Francis R. Elliott, Borden Co.
Robert L. Foreman, BBD & O
William H. Ewen, Borden Co.
William Hesse, Benton & Bowles
W. K. Eastman, S. C. Johnson
Earl Newsome
John Veckly, US Steel
McDonald Gillespie, BBD & O
B. E. Estes, Jr., US Steel
Anthony C. Chevins, Cunningham & Walsh
Kenneth Baumbusch, American Home Products
Edward H. Calhoun, Cunningham & Walsh
Melvin Hattwick, Continental Oil

Neal Gilliatt, McCann-Erickson
Paul Willis, Carnation Co.
Paul E. Foley, McCann-Erickson
Carl Watson, NBC
Lester Wunderman, Wunderman, Ricotta & Kline
Ralph Nunn, Maytag
Peter Hilton, Kastor, Hilton, Chesley, Clifford & Atherton
Albert R. Richardson, Chesbrough-Pond's
Edward L. Bernays
Harry W. Chesley, Jr., D'Arcy Advertising Co.
Bernard Tabbatt, Seagram
Maxwell Dane, Doyle Dane Bernbach
William A. Schneider, Corn Products
Richard K. Manoff, Richard K. Manoff
Jarlath J. Graham, *Advertising Age*
Charles Barry, Young & Rubicam
Richard LaBonte, McGraw Hill
Everett W. Hoyt, Charles Hoyt Co.
Alfred Whittaker, Bristol-Myers
Henry M. Schachte, J. Walter Thompson Co.
Lewis S. Rosensteil, Schenley
James J. McCaffrey, C. J. LaRoche & Co.
Howard J. Morgens, Procter & Gamble
George J. Callos, Klau-Van Pietersom-Dunlap
Anthony deLorenzo, General Motors
William A. Marsteller, Marsteller
R. A. Dobbin, Corn Products
Walter Seiler, Cramer-Krasseit
John Clampitt, United Airlines
Thomas B. Adams, Campbell-Ewald Co.
Peter D. Forsch, Nestle
Allen C. Smith, Jr., Aitkin-Kynett Co.
Howard Gray, R.J. Reynolds
William Henry, FCC
Paul Austin, Coca-Cola
Robert W. Boggs, Union Carbide
Vance Packard
Fred Borch, GE
Philip R. Warner, BBD & O
A. H. deGrassi, Kaiser Aluminum
John de Garmo, de Garmo
Phyllis Robinson, Doyle Dane Bernbach
Dan Seymour, J. Walter Thompson Co.
William E. Chambers, Jr., Foote, Cone & Belding
Richard C. Christian, Marsteller
Philip E. Bash, Clinton E. Frank
Wallace W. Elton, J. Walter Thompson Co.
William L. Spencer, Gardner Advertising Co.
William A. Bartel, West, Weir & Bartel
Herbert D. Strauss, Grey Advertising
C. Terence Clyne, Clyne, Maxon
William Mordwin, Hazard Advertising Co.
Peter G. Levathes, P. Lorillard
Ray Weber, Swift
B. David Kaplan, Norman, Craig & Kummel
Alfred Plant, Block Drug
Armando M. Sarmento, McCann-Erickson
Gerlad B. Zornow, Eastman Kodak
Esty Stowell, Ogilvy, Benson & Mather
J. Sanford Smith, GE
Arthur E. Tatham, Tatham-Laird & Kudner
Ralph P. Olmstead, Kellogg
Carl M. Post, Post-Keyes-Gardner
Ralston B. Reid, GE
Richard L. Gilbert, Gilbert Advertising

Sam Thurm, **Lever**
Ned Doyle, Doyle Dane Bernbach
Jane Wallace, Celanese
Earle Ludgin, Earle Ludgin & Co.
Walter Carlson, *New York Times*
Frank M. Hutchins, Hutchins Advertising Co.
Thomas J. Ross, Jr., American Airlines
Edward L. Bond, Jr., Young & Rubicam
James A. Linen III, Time, Inc.
Frank F. Morr, Post-Keyes-Gardner
Bill Tankersley, CBS
Robert E. Daiger, VanSant, Dugdale and Co.
Edward Kletter, J.B. Williams
Paul Brown, Al Paul Lefton Co.
John R. Bowers, Ford
Colin Campbell, Campbell-Ewald Co.
Richard Borden, Atlantic Refining
Kenneth G. Manuel, D. P. Brother & Co.
Robert J. Fisher, Ford
B. D. Adams, Adams, Burke, Dowling
John Toigo, Pepsi Cola
Chester T. Birch, Dancer-Fitzgerald-Sample
E. H. Lotspeich, Procter & Gamble
Jack Roberts, Carson/Roberts
Philip Hinerfeld, Pepsi Cola
Victor Bloede, Benton & Bowles
Henry W. Lowe, Warner Lambert
Joseph M. Greeley, Leo Burnett Co.
George C. Holtmann, Falstaff Brewing
Clifford L. Fitzgerald, Dancer-Fitzgerald-Sample

August A. Busch III, Anheuser Busch
Ralph Carson, Carson/Roberts
Edgar Bronfman, Seagram
Edward M. Thiele, Leo Burnett Co.
Richard S. Hait, Procter & Gamble
George Hammond, Carl Byoir
Max Banzhaf, Armstrong
Roger Bolin, Westinghouse
Joan Viedt, *New York Times*
A. N. Halverstadt, Procter & Gamble
Kenneth E. Moore, Fuller & Smith & Ross
J. Edward Dean, Dupont
Grace Johnson, ABC
Stuart D. Watson, McCann-Marschalk Co.
Donal O'Brien, Hiram Walker
George C. Reeves, J. Walter Thompson Co.
Manuel Yelen, P. Lorillard
James M. Henderson, Henderson Advertising
Richard L. Thomas, Gillette
Richard J. Farricker, Geyer, Morey, Ballard
Harry Schroeter, National Biscuit
Charles F. Adams, MacManus, John & Adams
Daniel Yankelovich
John H. Tinker, Jr., Jack Tinker and Partners
Robert Fearon, IBM
Jim Smith, *Chicago Tribune*
Thomas McCabe, Jr., Scott Paper
George Lois, Papert, Koenig, Lois
M. M. Masterpool, GE
R. W. Stafford, Knox Reeves Advertising

BIBLIOGRAPHY

I

Here follows a partial list of the books offered by the New York Public Library on advertising, marketing and related subjects. In considering whether to invest his time in reading any of them, the reader is reminded of the warnings on pages 117 and 118 of this volume.

Advertising, Kirkpatrick, C. A., Houghton Mifflin Co. 1964

Advertising, Davies, A. H., E. M. Hale & Co.

Advertising, Wright, S. S. and Warner, D. S., McGraw-Hill Book Co. 1962

Advertising, Dunn, S. W., Holt, Rinehart and Winston, Inc. 1961

Advertising, Field, E., McClelland

Advertising, Frey, A. W., Ronald Press Co. 1953

Advertising, Scott, S. D., Prentice-Hall, Inc. 1953

Advertising, A New Approach, Taplin, W., Little, Brown and Co. 1963

Advertising and the Public, Harris, R. and Seldon, A., André Deutsch 1962

Advertising in Action, Harris, R. and Seldon, A., Hutchinson 1962

Advertising in Action, Constantine, C. P., Superior Publications Co. 1962

Advertising Management, Wedding, N. and Lessler, R. S., Ronald Press Co. 1962

Advertising Principles and Problems, Dirksen, C. J. and Kroeger, A., Richard D. Irwin, Inc. 1964

Advertising: Today, Yesterday, Tomorrow, Printers' Ink, McGraw-Hill Book Co.

Advertising Theory and Practice, Sandage, C. H., Richard D. Irwin, Inc. 1963

Advertising and the Soul's Belly, Wood, P., University of Georgia Press 1961

Advertising: A General Introduction, Caplin, R. S., Business Publications (London) 1959

Advertising: Communications for Management, Crawford, J. W., Allyn and Bacon, Inc. 1960

Advertising in Modern Life, Gloag, J. E., William Heinemann, Ltd. 1959

Advertising Administration, Land, F. B., Butterworth & Co. 1962

Advertising: Creative Communication with Consumers, Hepner, H. W., McGraw-Hill Book Co. 1964

A History of English Advertising, Elliott, B. B., Batsford 1962

Advertising in a Free Society, Harris, R. and Seldon, A., Institute of Economic Affairs (London) 1959

Advertising: Mass Communications in Marketing, Kirkpatrick, C. A., Houghton Mifflin Co.

Advertising at Retail, Look, A., Golden Bell Press 1958

Advertising in America, Tyler, P., H. W. Wilson Co. 1959

Advertising Agency Success, Groesbeck, K., Harper & Row, Publishers, Inc. 1958

Answers to 317 Advertising Agency Problems, Groesbeck, K., Moore Publishing Co. 1958

Commercial Television, Sharps, W. S., Fountain Press, Morgan & Morgan, Inc., Publishers 1958

Colour in Advertising, Biggs, E., Studio (Technical) 1956

Casting for Advertising, Brandon, R., Bailey

Cooperative Advertising: The Way to Make It Pay, Hutchins, M. S., Ronald Press Co. 1953

Creative Advertising, Whittier, C. L., Holt, Rinehart and Winston, Inc. 1955

Effective Advertising, Solow, M. and Handman, E., Grosset & Dunlap, Inc. 1964

Bacon's Publicity Handbook, Bacon, R. H. & Co., The Company (Chicago)

Basic Text in Advertising, Davis, D. W., Printers' Ink 1955

Business Without Gambling, Cheskin, L., Quadrangle Books, Inc. 1963

Confessions of an Advertising Man, Ogilvy, D., Atheneum Publishers 1963

Cases in Advertising Management, Boyd, H. W. and others, McGraw-Hill Book Co. 1964

Call to Market, Knoble, C., McLeod 1963

Culture and Environment, Leavis, F. R. & Thompson, D., Barnes & Noble, Inc. 1964

Careers in Broadcasting, Lerch, J. H., Appleton-Century-Crofts, Inc. 1962

Casebook of Successful Ideas for Advertising and Selling, Baker, S. S., Doubleday & Co., Inc. 1959

Copywriting: Theory and Technique, Clarke, G. T., Harper & Row, Publishers, Inc.

Copywriting and Its Presentation, Jefkins, British Book Service

Copywriter's Guide, French, E. R., Harper & Row, Publishers, Inc.

Campaign Planning, Ellefson, O., Business Publications (London)

Clowns of Commerce, Goodman, W., Sagamore 1957

Culture and Environment, Leavis, F. R. and Thompson, D., Hillary House Publishers Ltd.

Advertising Techniques and Management, Zacher, R. V., Richard D. Irwin, Inc. 1961

Advertising Copywriting, Burton, P. W., Prentice-Hall, Inc. 1962

Animation Techniques and Commercial Film Production, Levitan, E. D., Reinhold Publishing Corp. 1962

Advertising to Business, Smith, R. B., Richard D. Irwin, Inc. 1957

Ads, Women and Boxtops, Jones, D., Printers' Ink 1955

Advertising Procedure, Kleppner, O., Prentice-Hall, Inc.

Advertising As a Service to Society, MacEwan, J., Sweetman 1956

America: Miracle at Work, Patterson, W., Prentice-Hall, Inc. 1953

Advertising and Research, Peerbhoy, A. S., Progressive Corp. 1964

Big Puff, Whiteside, T., Constable 1955

A Job in Television, Dunbar, J., Miss. Press 1961

Advertising Management: Text and Cases, Borden, N. H. and Marshall, M. V., Richard D. Irwin, Inc. 1959

Advertising Copy and Layout, Seil, M. D. and Senger, F. B., Interstate Printers & Publishers, Inc. 1959

Advertising Terminology, Grohman, H., Needham & Grohmann, Inc.

Advertising Media, Brown, L. O. and others, Ronald Press Co. 1957

Amazing Advertising Business, Fortune, Simon and Schuster, Inc. 1957

Advertising and Marketing to Young People, Gilbert, E., *Printers' Ink* 1957

Advertising and Psychology, Gill, L. E., Holt, Rinehart and Winston, Inc. 1954

Advertising in India, Mukherjee, Jiban, Calcutta

BIBLIOGRAPHY

II

HERE follows a most incomplete list of the books which have most influenced the author. Readers browse in these fields at their own risk.

Varieties of Religious Experience, William James

Studies in Classic American Literature, D. H. Lawrence

Love In the Western World, Denis de Rougement

The New York Times Style Book, Lewis Jordan

Elements of Style, W. Strunk and E. B. White

Signs of Life, H. M. Raphaelian

Irrational Man, William Barrett

The Theory of the Leisure Class, Thorstein Veblen

The True Believer, Eric Hoffer

The Art of Readable Writing, Rudolf Flesch

The Practical Cogitator, Curtis and Greenslet

The Public Philosophy, Walter Lippman

Memoirs of a Superfluous Man, Albert Jay Nock

The Last of the Wine, Mary Renault

In Defense of Sensuality, John Cowper Powys

A Common Place Book, Charles P. Curtis

John Brown's Body, Stephen Vincent Benet

Short Stories, Algernon Blackwood

The Fable, William Faulkner

Look Homeward, Angel, Thomas Wolfe

Collected Poems, Edna St. Vincent Millay

Straws and Prayer Books, James Branch Cabell

Beyond Life, James Branch Cabell

The Last Temptation of Christ, Nikos Kazantzakis

Point Counter Point, Aldous Huxley

Nausea, Jean-Paul Sartre

The Counterfeiters, André Gide

The Bridge on the Drina, Ivo Andric

Essays, Montaigne

Maxims, La Rochefoucauld

Catch-22, Joseph Heller

While Rome Burns, Alexander Woollcott

The Short Stories of Dorothy Parker

Arrowsmith, Sinclair Lewis

The Beautiful and Damned, F Scott Fitzgerald

The Sun Also Rises, Ernest Hemingway

The Light Guitar, Arthur Guiterman

The Hound of Heaven, Francis Thompson

Madison Avenue, Martin Mayer

The Knee-High Culture, Tom Griffith

The Hidden Persuaders, Vance Packard

The House of Intellect, Jacques Barzun

The Republic of Letters, Louis Kronenberger

The Craft of Fiction, Percy Lubbock

Mr. Blandings Builds His Dream House, Eric Hodgins

Man and Time, J. B. Priestley

Escape from Freedom, Erich Fromm

Magister Ludi, Hermann Hesse

All The Living, Henrietta Buckmaster

Collected Poems, e. e. cummings

The Fellowship of the Ring, John R. R. Tolkien

The Worm Ouroboros, E. R. Eddison

The Once and Future King, T. H. White

The Fairy Tales of Oscar Wilde

Pale Fire, Vladimir Nabokov

Riders in the Chariot, Patrick White

Principles of English Versification, P. F. Baum

The Affluent Society, John Kenneth Galbraith

The Lonely Crowd, David Riesman

Man Against Himself, Karl Menninger

Mistress Masham's Repose, T. H. White

The Stress of Life, Hans Selye

The Decline of Pleasure, Walter Kerr

The Twelve Seasons, Joseph Wood Krutch

The Human Condition, Hannah Arendt

The Joseph Tetralogy, Thomas Mann

The Sugar Pill, Thomas S. Matthews

African Genesis, Robert Ardrey

BIBLIOGRAPHY

III

HERE follows a partial list of books on advertising, marketing and related subjects not yet written but deserving, in the writer's opinion, an author, a publisher and a readership.

The Decline and Fall
of the Advertising Agency

Fire for Sale
The Nature and Value of the Creative Process in Business

Legacy of Guilt
Psychosomatic Attrition Among Advertising Executives

Humor and Power
A Study in Antipathy

The Pecking Order
in the Fourth Estate

Mammonoid and Tediophobe
An Approach to the Personnel Problem in Advertising

Red Sales in the Sunrise
Advertising in the USSR

The Image of the Image-Maker

The Motive
A Novel in Four Volumes
on the Reasons Why
Lorimer Jackson Switched Brands

Peanuts
or The Industrial Advertising Manager
and How He Shrank

Imagine Meeting You Here
or How Advertisers Change Agencies

Hunch, Punch and Howl
The Inside Story of How TV Programs are Rated

Self-Regulation
or A Step Ahead of Uncle Sam

Sex and the Single Ad Agency

Sinning Without Conception
or An Account Executive's Encounters with Grammar

Money Instead of Brains
or How To Snow a Market

INDEX

155

ENVOI

This book was designed by Laurence Lustig.
The text is set in Fairfield and the display face used
is Engravers Bold. The book is printed on Old Forge stock
with composition, printing and binding by
H. Wolff Book Manufacturing Co., New York